THE
ARCHITECTURE
OF *Motherhood*

YOUR BLUEPRINT
TO GLOW AS A
BUSINESS WOMAN
AND MOM

Kelly,
Thank you for the support!
I hope you enjoy this reading!

GLORIA KLOTER

Copyright © 2022 GLORIA KLOTER
Two Penny Publishing
850 E. Lime Street #266
Tarpon Springs, Florida 34688

TwoPennyPublishing.com
info@TwoPennyPublishing.com

All rights reserved. This book or parts thereof may not be reproduced in any form, stored in any retrieval system, or transmitted in any form by any means—electronic, mechanical, photocopy, recording, or otherwise—without prior written permission of the publisher, except as provided by United States of America copyright law.

Scriptures taken from the Holy Bible, New International Version®, NIV®. Copyright © 1973, 1978, 1984, 2011 by Biblica, Inc.™ Used by permission of Zondervan. All rights reserved worldwide. www.zondervan.com The "NIV" and "New International Version" are trademarks registered in the United States Patent and Trademark Office by Biblica, Inc.™

For permission requests and ordering information, email:
info@TwoPennyPublishing.com

Library of Congress Control Number: 2022909720

Paperback: 978-1-950995-71-4
eBook also available

FIRST EDITION

For information about this author, to book an event appearance or media interview, please contact the author representative at: info@ twopennypublishing.com

To all the *miracle makers*:

the marvelous women in architecture

and all other women in the workforce

who are mothers and mothers to be,

willing to navigate through the wonderfully

chaotic world of motherhood. You're the

bravest, most inspiring real-life heroines!

Table of Contents

Testimonials 7
Foreword 9
Preface 11
Chapter 1:   **H**appily Ever Architect 15
Chapter 2:   **O**nce Upon a Pregnancy 35
Chapter 3:   **W**elcome Pandemic Baby 49
Chapter 4:   **T**railblazing Calling 61
Chapter 5:   **O**wning a Business 77
Chapter 6:   **G**row Your Support System 99
Chapter 7:   **L**ead through Self-Awareness 121
Chapter 8:   **O**rganize the Chaos 137
Chapter 9:   **W**in by Grace 161
End Notes 175
Acknowledgments 177
About the Author 181

Testimonials

A beautiful story of the journey into this balancing act we call motherhood. Guided by faith and perseverance, Gloria's message is inspiring.

Joanna La Bounty

A beautiful read, full of vulnerability and encouragement to the mother's heart inside every woman. This book sheds light on successfully managing life as a mother and businesswoman in simple yet profound ways.

Lilian Boutros, AIA

Gloria's vulnerability with her struggles and fears is relatable, yet she turns each obstacle and disappointment into a strategy for motherhood and business, leaving the reader inspired that she can too.

Meggie Hoeft

An amazing story of resilience, faith, and compassion. Even though I'm not a mother, I learned so much about the business of Architecture and life-work balance.

Graciela Carrillo, AIA, LEED AP B+C.

Enlighted and uplifted. I felt as if a blindfold came off, at last, the thoughts in the heads of many women actually sounded different in writing. Coming directly from someone who did not want to choose one or the other (motherhood or to be a professional) and chose both; these thoughts now sound doable, because they are.

Jennifer Y. Bernal, MPA.

I absolutely loved this book. I too have often stressed myself about the balance between motherhood and my career—When should I start? Am I successful enough to have a kid? How much is a child going to set me back in my career? These questions are constantly flooding my head, more so lately. This book helped give me a lot of assurance. It's a quick, inspirational read to let women know they really can have it all!

Brittany Baldwin, AIA, NCARB.

A genuine and thoughtful approach to a challenge many career women face. Gloria's insights have already had such a positive impact on how I balance my own personal and career goals.

Holley Madderra Cornell

Foreword

As an architect and a mother, I wish this book by Gloria Kloter- *The Architecture of Motherhood* had been around when I had my children many years ago. Gloria does a fantastic job of describing the challenges that all professional women face when thinking about motherhood and how it will affect their professional lives.

She beautifully describes her journey as a student and architect in her home country of the Dominican Republic, and how she transitioned to becoming an architect in the United States after falling in love with her husband.

Her faith in God and herself have guided her through the trials and tribulations of becoming a registered architect in Florida, becoming a mother, and finally becoming a business owner. Her grasp of how fear can stop us and how to fight our own self-doubts is evident throughout the book. Her ability to help herself and others has made her a leader in the architecture profession.

Now with this book, she can also help emerging professionals who may not think that being a mother and an architect is possible. This was a concept that my generation did not even envision because we fought so hard to be in the profession in the first place; just because we had children was not going to stop us from doing what we loved and worked so hard to achieve.

Gloria provides great tools and suggestions so that we can all create our own journeys with confidence, faith, strength, courage, and willingness to ask for help.

Embracing change is important and when there is a will, there is a way to achieve our goals. Thank you, Gloria, for taking the time to share your experiences so that others can learn and glow from them.

Lourdes Solera, FAIA
Managing Principal, MCHarry & Associates, Inc. - Architects

Preface

Have you ever been afraid of starting a family and how it would impact your professional life? I have.

> I was once afraid that motherhood would force me to pause—or entirely stop—my architectural career.

In its 2020 annual report, the National Architectural Accrediting Board (NAAB) revealed that 50% of the 26,977 students enrolled in NAAB-accredited architecture programs—B. Arch, M. Arch, and D. Arch—were female.[1]

This is a number that has been improving since the 1970s, yet the percentage of women who obtain their architect license, achieve upper management positions, become partners and own architectural firms have not increased at the same rate as men have. To date, data from the National Council of Architectural Registration Boards (NCARB) 2021 by the Numbers report shows that only 24% of the 121,997 registered architects in the United States are female.[2]

Why is there such a gap?

Based on these facts, I was worried that if I started to grow my family, then it would be the death of my career. On top of it—and like most women experience—I was continuously pressured with unsolicited advice and opinions on how I needed to start having kids early and how as a woman, I should have a family or a career, not both.

Many conversations around me implied an unspoken shame and a sense of guilt in wanting to still have a professional career after having kids. "Why would you want to keep working?! Aren't you planning to have kids?!"—Someone once asked me, horrified after hearing about my professional aspirations when I got married.

I was also once told that if I would try to take these two roles at the same time, I was going to fail at one of the two, or at both. It was important to choose between one role or the other, and focus on being successful at that single one. Period. Yet, there was a part of me that couldn't accept this theory entirely. *There had to be a better way.*

I love being an architect and a woman in the workforce, and I recklessly longed for—with every cell of my existence—to be a mother. In my heart, architecture and motherhood are so similar.

I have always defined architecture as a creative miracle, and mothers are miracle makers.

God made no mistakes creating us in this incredible way.

I never understood why two worlds that feel so comparable in nature, seemed to be impossible to coexist at the same time in the life of a woman. In reality, we women are limitless, held back only by what we believe we can accomplish. It's within ourselves to take a step forward and make things happen.

I decided I was going to go against the grain. I was going to find a balance between architecture and motherhood, shine light over the shadows and myths holding me back, and *glow* as a successful, professional woman and mother—and hopefully, show others how they could *glow* too.

We are without a doubt marvelous.

Only women hold the power to create and bring life into the world.

We're vessels from God, reflect on that for a moment and let it sink in. As a woman, YOU CAN CREATE LIFE. Do you know how powerful you are? How amazing this power is? Women are extraordinary beings, and we **deserve** to follow our hearts and passions in our professional life, while still raising a family. One path in life should not be justifiable over the other—no matter what the stereotypes are. Women deserve to have it all.

"While architecture is considered the mother of all arts, *Women* are the mothers of all civilization."

Gloria Kloter

Chapter 1

Happily Ever Architect

The level of sacrifices I've made for my love of architecture shaped me into the professional I am today. Every career path comes with its unique challenges.

> **I gave everything to earn the privilege of calling myself an architect.**

My career is important to me, and because you're reading this book, I know for a fact that your career is important to you too.

I've always been certain of my desire to become a mother, but there was a time when I felt afraid of starting to grow my family. I was concerned with the thought that by doing so I was going to limit my professional development, and I was never going to be the successful architect I envisioned. I was wrong, I just didn't know it at the time. I wish I did.

This is a struggle many other women in the workforce deal with throughout their professional journey. If you're asking yourself: Do I have to give up on my career in order to be a successful mother? Or do I have to give up on motherhood in order to be a successful professional?

The answer to both is: No, you don't.

The value you bring to the table and the way you contribute to society as a professional matters. There's no reason to feel guilt or shame about wanting to be a career-oriented woman while raising a family. There are ways to find a balance between both worlds. So brace yourself, sister, and read on! Because I'm going to share with you how I figured this whole thing out, and how you can do it too.

Little Architect in the Making

Growing up, I wasn't one of those lucky children who always knew what they wanted to be as an adult. Adulthood seemed very far away to me, and I just focused on the things I enjoyed. However, there was one thing I was certain of, I knew one day I wanted to become a mom.

My mother and father divorced when I was five, and because of it, growing up we didn't have much money. Yet, I love and admire my mother for everything she did for herself, and for my sister and me. My mom worked very hard to give us the best life she could, and even from a young age, I understood to some level the sacrifices she made to provide for us.

Although she worked incredibly hard, things were tight for us for a long time, and because of it, I didn't have a lot of toys and accessories most young girls would usually have. However, I still found ways to enjoy myself and made full use of my imagination.

> **I believe the lack of resources influenced me to develop higher levels of creativity, which enabled me to enjoy many things over the course of my childhood.**

I fell in love with art, poetry, and drawing in particular. I had a love for things anyone could look at and appreciate. So, while other children would talk about what they wanted to be when they grew up, I never really had a set idea of where I wanted to be in the future. I was just enjoying each day at a time, and I tried to do it to the fullest.

I noticed how lots of little girls around me just pretended to play with dolls and to be the dolls' mothers. While that was something I enjoyed doing as well, it wasn't the only thing I liked.

As a child, I would often create spaces for my dolls, almost like little rooms. My mother saw me playing one day and noticed how much I enjoyed making rooms for each of my dolls, so she bought me a wooden headboard to fit at the end of my bed that had shelves and slots on it.

I was ecstatic! Each one of the shelves was a different size, which was perfect. I imagined every single one was a different room for my dolls and I decorated them accordingly—creating places and custom furniture for my dolls to live, work, raise babies, and have all kinds of adventures.

Although I enjoyed creating spaces for my dolls, I still loved to play *mother* as well. So, deep down there was always a part of me that had a maternal instinct. Looking back, I realized I had a talent for architecture and interior design. Yet, as a child little did I know this passion would blossom as I grew and discovered more about it.

In fact, even though I was naturally gifted in architecture and loved it from a young age, I actually started pursuing it by pure coincidence.

A friend of mine, and neighbor, started her studies in architecture school long before I did. Despite the fact that I was still in high school and she had begun going to college, I would visit her house very frequently.

I was always so fascinated with her architectural design homework, and I could clearly see different ways to solve the problems she was given in school. In addition to being talented in architecture, I was also a great problem-solver, which is a skill great architects have, and one I would later utilize on a daily basis.

Ironically enough, my neighbor and friend did not stick with architecture. Instead, she ended up switching careers and became a successful psychologist in the Dominican Republic. Yet, for me, after becoming interested in just one small part of it, I ended up giving architecture a try and I never looked back.

Due to the lack of money and my parent's divorce, I had to work hard for every little thing I accomplished in life, including all my academic achievements.

> **Being someone who grew up having to work hard for everything, architecture became the means for me to express myself as an individual, artist, and creator.**

Architecture made me feel powerful. I could bring things into this world in a way it hadn't been brought before, full of life, certainty, and opportunities. It was amazing to create buildings, knowing how their future was unlimited.

Architecture helped me escape from anything and everything broken in my life, but it also helped me appreciate things on a deeper and more meaningful level. I was able to look at buildings and see where their stories began and imagine how they would evolve. Buildings change and adapt with their surroundings, just as human beings do.

Do You Believe In Destiny?

It was 2009 and I was excited to finish college. I was approaching my final semester at last and it felt like my life was going in the direction that it was meant to be. As I was walking home, I remembered one of my friends hadn't given some books back following a study group we had, so I decided to visit his house to pick them up.

My friend greeted me at the door and asked me to wait in the living room as he fetched them. While I was there, his aunt greeted me politely. Then, she said something I wasn't expecting.

"I have a message for you," she stated.

I nodded politely and looked towards the door for my friend who had not yet returned. I felt it was a bit of a strange thing to say and hoped my friend would hurry up.

"God wants me to tell you something about your future," she continued. I was not a believer at the time of anything in particular, especially anything prophetic, and this lady made me feel anxious. I wanted to run out of their home and get back to my studies.

However, I did not wish to be impolite; I nodded and smiled, gesturing for her to continue.

To my surprise, she then came over to me, lightly patting me on the shoulder, and said:

> "He wants you to wait. He has revealed to me the image of a tall, white man. He is dressed in a military uniform. God wants you to know that this man will love you in a way you will never comprehend, greater than any other man.

He showed me US dollars instead of Dominican pesos. In your future, you'll be traveling around the world, speaking in front of crowds in another language, and helping many individuals like yourself…"

As much as I tried to hold it back, I couldn't help it and started laughing at her; it seemed a little too ridiculous for me to wrap my head around.

"I have never traveled outside of the Dominican Republic, I don't even have a visa to visit the US or any other country. How would I travel around the world?! I also don't know any tall, white military men. Never mind one who could love me in the way you described. I don't believe this, I'm sorry!" I said to her, rolling my eyes and shaking my head.

Then she squinted at me and smiled in a strange, knowing way.

> "I see it very clearly, though. You'll marry this man and you'll have a daughter together.

She will be so beautiful and bright, she will be a light to many. God wants you to believe and wait for Him. Give your heart to Christ and surrender," she said, and her smile grew wider.

Luckily, before I was forced to endure anything further, my friend appeared and handed me the books I needed. I said my goodbyes to both him and his aunt, and then went on my way.

On my way home, I began to ponder her predictions—being loved in a way I couldn't comprehend, getting married, having a family, traveling around the world, and having a child! Giving my life to Christ? It all felt so ridiculous—I wasn't a believer, I hadn't finished my studies yet, and I was single at the time.

That was so strange! What a load of rubbish! I thought to myself and then giggled, shrugging the whole weird experience off. I forgot about the whole thing not too long after.

By this time, I had a couple of failed romantic relationships, and because of it, I ended up staying single for a while by choice. I was focused on my career, pouring my heart and soul into my studies and my job. I decided architecture would come first, rather than pursuing anything else.

To me, everything else pales in comparison; I was determined to succeed. *I had to succeed.*

When the Opportunity Meets Preparation

Not long after that strange prophetic event, I graduated. I'm originally from the Dominican Republic, so it was there that I received my bachelor's degree in architecture. Following this, I received a master's in architecture design with an emphasis on architecture of interiors, which qualified as being a double degree from both the Dominican Republic and Spain.

I started an architecture studio in Santo Domingo once I was fully qualified. I specialized in both residential and commercial projects, particularly in retail stores. Everything was exciting and promising. I was a new architect in the field, with many years of experience—as I had to work hard since the very beginning of my career—and I was ready to put my mark on the world. I also became a professor of architectural drafting and design at a well-known design school in the Dominican Republic, Chavón.

> **Then almost as quickly as I had set up my architecture studio, I was given an amazing opportunity.**

I was asked to design and build the first Steve Madden in the Dominican Republic, a designer shoe retail store that set my architectural work apart from the crowd. The project was published by Arquitexto, one of the biggest architectural journals in my home country. It was an incredible opportunity and it opened so many other doors in my career.

Working on this project was everything I dreamed of when I started my architectural business journey, having something set in stone that you've designed and built, rooms in which people were able to literally walk inside of. It was no longer just in my head, but now others could finally see, touch, smell, and experience it in their own way.

> A space where the general public would enjoy for generations. A space that was mine. Forever.

What a euphoric feeling!

Completing the project was in itself everything I had wanted and desired—I was finally putting my mark on the world after years of hard work and dedication.

After designing the store, getting published in Arquitexto was just the icing on the cake. The attention I got following the publication helped to skyrocket my career and it brought me many more retail, commercial, and residential projects. I was busy, my business was growing, and most importantly I was happy; I felt like I was living the dream.

Then, I met him.

Love at First Dance

Jeremy was a Marine at the time, and he was stationed at the US Embassy located in Haiti. We met in 2013 when he came to visit the Dominican Republic for the first time.

Even though it will sound like such a cliché, it was love at first sight, or better said, at first dance, as we met in a club and we danced all night long.

He was gorgeous, tall, and strong, yet he had the cutest face and most charming smile. I remember thinking he was incredibly handsome and far out of my league. I imagined he would never pursue a serious relationship with me, as he quite literally took my breath away.

> **After all this time focusing solely on my career rather than relationships, I felt vulnerable and somewhat out of control.**

I gazed at him with awe and felt my heart hammer when I first laid eyes on him. *He's not going to even entertain the thought of being with someone like me*—I thought to myself.

Thank God, I was wrong.

We met and it was like we had known each other forever. We fit together like nothing else I had ever known before, and we started dating not too long after meeting. Being around Jeremy was so easy. He became my safe place, a drama-free zone, and a source of peace and happiness. We spent every moment we could together, and we were like two peas in a pod.

I had never met someone before whom I could imagine spending my life with, but every moment with him felt better than anything I had ever experienced before. There was no pain, fear, or doubts when I was around him, only love, peace and happiness. Every second I spent with him, it was as if there were a thousand butterflies swimming in my stomach.

For the very first time in my life, I felt truly loved by a man.

Giving My Life to Christ

Soon after we started dating, he invited me to Florida and introduced me to his wonderful family. I remember it as if it was yesterday.

It was October of 2013. I was talking with Jeremy's mom in her kitchen, sitting behind the countertop while she was making dinner. That year she celebrated 33 years of marriage with Jeremy's dad, and I said:

"I come from a broken family, my parents got divorced when I was five years old. It amazes me how you raised five wonderful boys and stayed happily married all these years… How did you do it?" I asked.

To my surprise, her answer was very simple:

> **"Well… The truth is, you just need to have Jesus as the center of your life and marriage, and He takes care of the rest."**

Her words made such an impact on me. It felt as if a knife went through my chest and cut it wide open. I couldn't stop thinking about it. I wanted the stability, peace, and love she had, and she literally shared with me the key to her success. She became a role model to me and someone I looked up to with admiration in so many ways.

I returned back home on a Saturday, and I gave my life to Christ the next day on Sunday, October 13, 2013.

My faith transpired at the perfect time. It grew stronger as I learned more about Jesus. It became my anchor and shield when

I was going through trials and tribulations later in life. My faith was ultimately what kept me grounded. God had a plan for me. I just didn't know it yet.

Starting Over

Before I knew it, two wonderful years passed by with Jeremy and it felt like I had found the one I wanted to spend the rest of my life with. Eventually, we got married in 2015 and decided to move, starting our new life together in Tampa, Florida.

By the time we married, he had left the Marines and started a business in real estate. I was very successful in the field of architecture and was excited to bring my talents to the USA. However, I found I was not able to start my own architecture firm in the USA as they viewed architectural licenses differently.

I was shocked! I had the credits, certifications, and experience to prove I was able to design and build incredible things, yet in the eyes of the United States, it was almost as if I had never obtained an architect license before.

So, as much as I hated the idea of becoming an employee again, I had to take a job at an architecture firm. If I wanted to run my own architecture business again, I would have to go on a new journey to transfer my architecture license to the US.

This was a long, draining, and grueling path, and one I struggled with greatly. The paperwork required to be filled out upfront to validate my experience and education was confusing and complicated, and because of the challenges right at the very start, I knew there were going to be many more hurdles along the way.

As the paperwork was quite daunting, I eventually opted for a path tailored for foreign licensed architects—people who were already qualified in the field of architecture in other countries. Following this, I began studying for the Architect Registration Exams (also known as ARE). However, I found this process was infuriating.

I had studied immensely hard all my life in the field of architecture and was well-known for the things I had designed back home. I had designed spaces that would last for decades to come. Yet in America, it felt like I was back to square one and had hit rock bottom. I almost felt like a student going to college all over again, working hard towards her future.

All my accomplishments didn't seem to matter in the eyes of America and it absolutely killed me inside.

There's a lot of pride involved in calling yourself an architect, and as I was no longer allowed to do so, my pride was completely destroyed and vanished.

I was not seen as the renowned architect and professor of design I was, everything I had worked so hard for my entire life meant nothing.

Although at the time, it all felt like the end of the world to me, looking back I do not regret going through the entire process as I did. God works in mysterious ways. Even though it was an extremely hard time in my life, in the end, this experience made me a better architect and I met the most wonderful people on this journey, with many of them being like family now.

What doesn't kill us makes us stronger, right? This was the case for me.

Delaying a Family

Although Jeremy and I knew we wanted children at some point in our marriage, we knew we were building each other's careers up and we didn't feel ready yet to start having babies. So, we had to put a hold on it amidst the chaos of gaining my architectural license, and Jeremy growing his businesses. I was very ambitious and so was he, and our careers were very important to us.

While I wanted to believe I was able to excel at both—motherhood and architecture—deep inside of me I was afraid I was not capable of it, and I thought at that moment in time I needed to wait. I kept telling myself how I wanted to be able to fully enjoy any pregnancy I would have, and to be exclusively focused on the experience, as I always believed it was quite unique.

> **And it is, but what I didn't know was I didn't need to stop my entire life in order to enjoy a pregnancy.**

Because of this misconception of things in my head, I decided to sort out my architecture license first, and then I could wrap my head around the thought of creating a family with my husband.

Jeremy and I managed to spend a lot of quality time together and check off several items on our bucket list. We enjoyed each other's company and spent as much time as possible together. We had lots of adventures and created many wonderful memories, which I would not trade for anything. Although taking the Architect Registration Exams (ARE) was a time in my life incredibly frustrating, Jeremy and I were able to make the best out of it and enjoy life, appreciate the simple things around us, and I still to this day treasure it all greatly.

Crossing the Finish Line

After what felt like a lifetime, in 2019 I obtained my architect license in Florida. Everything had finally fallen into place, life was good, Jeremy's businesses were doing well, and I was able to call myself an architect again.

We had purchased a house and two puppies. We were ready to move forward with the next items on our bucket list, and achieve the rest of our personal and professional goals. After talking about it, although both of us were eager to start trying for children, we decided to have one last adventure with just the two of us.

> **Although both of us were eager to start trying for children, we decided to have one last adventure with just the two of us.**

We wanted to travel to Europe and the UK, it was one of those big items on our bucket lists we hadn't gotten around to over the last few years. Because of this, we delayed having children for just a little longer. Most of our family and friends would usually try to conceive between six months to a year before getting pregnant, so we decided we would start trying to conceive during our travels, this way we could plan on getting pregnant the year after.

We purchased the flight tickets, booked all the hotels, and off we went. We traveled to Barcelona first, arriving on

September 22, 2019. We visited several cities in Spain, France, Italy, and finally in the UK.

I thought at that point in life I had it all. Little did I know the best was yet to come.

Many women in all avenues of business struggle with the thought of growing their families and the impact it may have on their careers. I know this very well, especially because I lived it in the flesh myself, and because I'm surrounded by other amazing women in the professional world who have expressed similar feelings. I see them. I see you. You're not alone.

At the time, I didn't fully understand how—or even if—I was able to handle both architecture and motherhood. I was not willing to give up on my career, not then and not now, and I felt sometimes guilty for not wanting one over the other. They were equally important to me.

I want to acknowledge those who feel the same way. Do you feel this way too? If your answer is yes, just know you're not alone. My prayer is that my story makes you feel empowered, knowing it's ok to want to be a successful professional and that there's no shame in feeling this way.

> **While architecture is considered the mother of all arts, women are the mothers of all civilization.**

You've earned the right to love your professional career as well as your personal goals.

YOUR TURN:

1. What is your why?

   _____
   _____

2. Why is your career important to you?

   _____
   _____

3. What did you go through to get to where you're at right now in your professional life?

   _____
   _____

4. Why is it important to you to be a successful professional, despite your personal goals with motherhood?

   _____
   _____

TAKEAWAYS:

- Your career and professional development matter.
- It's ok to be proud of who you are as a professional.
- Being a successful professional won't mean you'll be a bad mother, and motherhood won't mean the end of your career.
- It's ok to take your time to make life-changing decisions.
- It's your journey, not anyone else's.

Draw Your Thoughts

"I didn't comprehend *life* until I created one with my own body."

Gloria Kloter

Chapter 2

Once Upon a Pregnancy

There's something sacred about a woman's body and its ability to create life. Some women even feel a maternal instinct from a very young age. I was one of them. I longed for the magic, the unmeasurable love, and the incomparable bond a mother shares with her baby. I wanted the *glow*. But my fear to disrupt the advancement of my professional world convinced me to delay pursuing such an extraordinary and unique experience.

What's funny was my ignorance in understanding that there are things in life we can't plan with exact accuracy, because they are beyond the scope of our control. Only God can control them.

> **They are beyond the scope of our control. Only God can control them.**

Sometimes things can take way longer than we expected, sometimes things will come way sooner than we anticipated. What truly matters is our ability to adapt when we're hit by the reality of things, being able to thrive while shifting priorities back and forth, and finding ways to keep *glowing* as we navigate through it all moving forward.

The Euro-Trip of My Life

It was a Thursday morning, October 3, 2019, and I awoke before my husband. The air was crisp, and outside on the streets of London the trees glimmered with hints of orange, gold, and brown indicating we were truly into fall. Halloween was gradually approaching and the haze of being on vacation was starting to drift away.

We had a flight back to Tampa after the most beautiful two weeks of our vacation together. It had been so incredible spending this time traveling, just the two of us. It was a well-deserved—and very much needed - time off and away from everything.

That morning, I wanted to get up early to make sure everything was in order and ready for us to leave. Our vacation had come to its end and as someone who was always organized and eager to get going, I was up first.

I started brushing my teeth when all of a sudden, the cool bristles of the toothbrush touched my tongue a wave of nausea hit me.

It was not the usual vacation sickness you would feel from something you ate; it was… different.

I looked at my husband, who was still fast asleep in bed and breathing softly; he always looked so peaceful and content when he slept. It was almost angelic in a way and I smiled to myself as I watched him.

Yet, as I looked at him, unusual nausea hit me again, and a thought swam through my mind:

> *There's no freaking way.*

Shock ran through me; *could I really be pregnant this fast?*—I thought—*There's no way!*—I repeated to myself.

We hadn't tried much towards the end of our travels, although we had both agreed it was time to start trying for children. Yet, I didn't think anything like it could happen so fast. *Nobody gets pregnant that quick*—I continued to tell myself.

Quickly, I shook it off as impossible, presuming I had just eaten something the night before which may have upset my stomach. I probably was just overthinking it. After all, we had spent a long time traveling and British food was quite different from American food. *Yes, it was probably something I ate. I'm sure I'll feel better by the time I get home.* I put it out of my mind and began packing. It was different, yes, but it only lasted a few seconds anyway, so at that point, I was certain the whole thing meant nothing.

We got ready and set out to go back home to Tampa. We had a long nine-hour flight ahead of us. I was used to traveling a lot with my husband, but when we finally arrived back home, I felt nauseous again.

"It's probably something you ate, combined with the long flight." Jeremy stated as we got back to Tampa and were on our way home.

Yet, the more I turned it around in my mind, it didn't quite make sense. It just felt so… different.

We decided to pick up a pregnancy test from the local store on our way home, and I would take it the following morning. I was so anxious about it I ended up buying three pregnancy tests instead of just one. Although a part of me was sure I wasn't pregnant, I just wanted to confirm it.

When we got home, I spent most of the night wide awake unable to sleep.

> **Could this really be happening? Was it possible I'm carrying a life inside of me already? Was I really on the path to becoming a mother?**

We haven't been trying that long, we barely started trying about two weeks ago… don't these things usually take longer?

The thoughts swirled around my mind all night at a maddening pace, and eventually, I couldn't bear staring up at the ceiling any longer.

I turned my attention to my phone next to our bed and touched the screen to reveal the time. *October 4, 2019. 6:00 AM.*

I got out of bed slowly, feeling both nervous and excited all rolled into one tangled emotion. *Here goes nothing.*

I took one pregnancy test, yet I wasn't sure of what I was looking at when I finished using it. I stared at it but couldn't tell the reading as it was very faded. It showed what seemed to me only one dark pink bar, and the second test came out the same; indicating I wasn't pregnant.

I must admit, as scared as I was the day before, I was quite disappointed to see one single dark pink bar on both pregnancy tests.

One test remained. The third test was different from the first two. It was a digital pregnancy test, which assured to detect pregnancy as early as five days over the other brands. In particular, this one spelled out the words "pregnant or not pregnant' very clearly. I stared at it; it felt like something inside of me was pulling me towards it, begging me to just try one last time.

"I guess it can't hurt," I said to myself and then used it.

I waited for something to come up on the screen after I was finished and stared at it for what felt like an eternity. There were little loading bars on the screen to show it was analyzing whether I was pregnant or not.

Why does it take so long? This one is quite different from the other tests. Interesting. I thought to myself while feeling somewhat discouraged and defeated.

Those three minutes felt like the longest minutes of my life. Suddenly, the bars went full after what seemed like forever, the screen got blank for a second, and then one word flashed up on the screen in all caps:

PREGNANT

"What?!" It was the most terrifying, yet exciting word I have ever read in my life. Time stopped for a second as I read the word over and over and over again as if I was afraid it was going to change or disappear or say something different.

Yet the word remained there, telling me I was in fact pregnant. I felt like pinching myself as I wondered for a moment if there was a chance I was still asleep and hadn't checked it at all.

I entered into some state of shock; I remained standing in the cool bathroom and stared at the screen. *This was real. I really was pregnant. Oh my God, this was really happening!* I had thought excitedly.

Heat rose up my body, from my feet to my neck, my ears, and finally to the top of my head making me feel a little dizzy. My hands began to shake and tears rolled down my cheeks as the reality of the situation began to set in.

"Oh, God… Oh, God… Oh, God!" I whispered, in shock.

For me, **in that instant I became a mother**. I knew I would do anything and everything in my power to protect this little life growing inside of me; my baby was now my number one priority.

I'm a mother. I said to myself.

Of course, my career and professional dreams were still important but suddenly, everything else just felt like it fell into the background, it went blurry on a third plane. I was having a child, and nothing was more important than the little life I would one day meet.

I grabbed the three tests in my hand and ran into our bedroom. Jeremy was already up, sitting at the edge of the bed waiting for me. He looked at me as tears ran down my cheeks, my hands were shaking, and words couldn't get out of my mouth. He raised an eyebrow, and with a smile on his face he asked:

"Are we having a little croissant?"

When Destiny Reaches Peak

A few weeks after we found out we were expecting, we decided to celebrate a gender reveal together with our family and closest friends.

Jeremy held the rifle in his arms and slowly looked down the iron sight as he adjusted his position slightly. I looked at him with a sense of wonder and awe, happiness swimming in my heart with the thought of him soon becoming a father.

He was targeting a box filled with colored powder, located about 100 yards away. Our friend put it together for us just a couple of minutes before, so she was the only one there who knew what we were having. We were seconds from finding out our baby's gender, and I was ecstatic with the thought. We had both been eager to learn the gender since I had found out I was pregnant, and now it was finally time to see once and for all whether we were having a girl or a boy.

Behind us, there were about 40 people who were also anxious to find out what we were having, close friends and family members all watching eagerly as Jeremy poised himself, ready to shoot the box. I was standing next to him, my heart thumping loudly in my chest. For a moment, I was certain everyone could hear my heartbeat with how loud it was.

Was it a girl? Was it a boy?

I thought while my heart raced more and more by the second—It felt as if it was going to explode out of my chest.

Then, as the sound of my own heartbeat overpowered and muted all the background noise around me, the prophetic words from the lady I had met back in 2009 swam to me—my old friend's aunt. I had forgotten about her until now. *Maybe she was onto something after all? This all does seem eerily similar to what she said.* I thought.

I had ended up marrying a military man who happened to be tall and white, just like the woman had predicted. And the man truly loved me in a way, unlike anything I had ever known, not to mention in a way I felt was beyond measure. I had moved to the USA and had been traveling around the world with my husband, and by this time, I also started doing keynote presentations at different architecture conferences and mentoring many foreign architects like myself to obtain their architect license in the USA as well.

Now… Now I was pregnant and seconds away from finding out our baby's gender!

> **Oh my God, what if she was right and I'm having a girl?!**

Now that I think about it, everything else she said came true! I thought to myself excitedly.

Then I looked at our friend who prepared the colored powder box for us, as she was serving a colored lemonade for herself. We prepared pink and blue drinks for people to display their vote on the baby's gender. She picked the blue one. At that exact second, I knew we were having a boy. There was a part of me that felt disappointed. I wanted to believe everything the lady once told me about my future was truly a message from God, but it seemed like she wasn't completely right after all, we were having a boy. "In the end what matters is that he's ours, healthy and loved," I said to myself.

I stayed quiet. Even though I saw how our friend served herself a blue drink, I knew Jeremy didn't notice it, so I didn't want to spoil it for him too.

I was amazed by how Jeremy was able to stay so calm and collected, despite the number of people behind us watching and me at his side. It was a lot of pressure on his shoulder to be quite honest, but as the saying goes—Once a marine, always a marine… OORAH!

Jeremy took a deep breath, then slowly exhaled all the air out, and in the midst of the quietness offered by that single second, everything just stopped, and he pulled the trigger.

> **Time seemed to slow as the bullet exploded from the gun and shot towards the target.**

Although it was less than a second until it hit the box, it felt like forever as we watched it in anticipation. I can still remember it as if it was all in slow motion before my eyes.

Jeremy had an excellent shot though, and the bullet went straight into the bullseye symbol on the first try. The box exploded in the air, and a loud BOOM rippled through everyone's ears. I gasped as a huge cloud of smoke enveloped the sky and the air around us. It felt magical; the sky above us was no longer blue. It was now covered by a mystical pink. Yes, you read it right, IT WAS PINK!

I bet my friend served herself the blue drink purposely to deceive me, and I totally fell for it!

We were having a girl! Of course, we had already settled on a name for either gender—just in case. Yet, it all seemed to fit together so perfectly and I smiled to myself at the thought of meeting her soon. *Our baby girl, Nova Isabella*—Which together means "The creation of a star, devoted to God."

It was also fascinating for me to think of how ten years ago the lady told me God revealed all of these things to her, how all of this would happen in my life, and I just didn't believe it. She was right, every word was true, and my whole self was thankful to God for it.

The truth is, things didn't happen within the timeline we planned and prepared for, and this was just the beginning of a chain of unplanned events that came our way.

> **I didn't comprehend life until I created one with my own body.**

A mother's body is sacred and precious. The complexity of what our bodies go through during pregnancy is just mind-blowing. God has chosen us women for such a divine task and His timing is perfect.

Dear mama, it doesn't matter if your pregnancy was planned or it happened unexpectedly fast like mine, if it came after lots of unsuccessful trying, or if motherhood showed up in your life as a complete surprise. Know that creating life on its own is a miracle, and being a mother, whether you birthed your baby or not, is a privilege. Even what you experience from trying to conceive one pregnancy to another can look so different. Only God knows the perfect timing for things. Don't take the time to start your motherhood journey for granted.

YOUR TURN:

1. When was the last time that something unexpected happened in your life and it turned out to be a blessing?

   _____
   _____

2. When you're faced with a new challenge, how do you react to it?

   _____
   _____

3. Whether you're a mother or a mother-to-be, why is motherhood important to you?

   _____
   _____

4. How do you think motherhood could change your professional career for the better?

   _____
   _____

TAKEAWAYS:

- Women have been chosen by God. We are more powerful than we realize.
- Motherhood starts at conception, pregnancy is a blessing, and creating life is a miracle and a privilege.
- It's ok to let your priorities shift, move, and evolve as life happens.
- Wherever you're at now in life, know it's because God planned this ahead of time for you, and His plans are always better than ours.

Draw Your Thoughts

"Babies are *light* in its purest form, bright enough to make a glare in the darkest of circumstances."

Gloria Kloter

Chapter 3

Welcome Pandemic Baby

Sometimes the hardest conditions can bring out the best of you. Diamonds are made under pressure and heat. Going through dark circumstances will show you what you're really made of, your resiliency, adaptability, strength, and power.

Motherhood is transformational.

It converted me into someone greater than I ever was before. It will do the same for you, no matter how uncertain your situation may be.

Into the Darkness

To my surprise, my pregnancy was very different from what I anticipated. I was excited to spend time planning out things with my family and having them meet my daughter as soon as she was born.

Although the baby and I were healthy throughout the pregnancy, something else came up and turned the entire world upside down. COVID-19 began to creep up on every single continent, including America.

Coronavirus came and rocked the whole world mercilessly. I remember watching the news and hearing about it when it first broke out in Wuhan. It seemed unbelievable to me that one illness could turn a whole city upside down. In fact, at the time I couldn't help but wonder if some of it was exaggerated. So, I shrugged it off after reading about it; presuming this mysterious illness would disappear from the news in about a week or so like other articles tended to do.

As you know, I was wrong.

Slowly, the virus crept toward America and the rest of the world. Everyone, including myself, was shocked at how country after country succumbed to its dark grasp. There were many unknowns at the time, and the way the little information available was being delivered to the population only created a sense of fear and uncertainty in every single soul. Governments forced lockdowns around the world, and the death toll seemed to skyrocket. I couldn't quite believe how fast it had traveled around the world and how everywhere seemed to change so quickly.

In fact, it shocked me how in this day and age a pandemic could break out and rock the world like this so much.

Fear took over our freedom, and all of our plans were forcefully changed by it.

It was heartbreaking in a lot of ways. This was my first pregnancy and I had to cancel events leading up to Nova being born, to celebrate her arrival. All my family and friends had their flights to visit us canceled. My parents and siblings couldn't see me in person at all while I was pregnant. There are no photos of me next to my mom with her hands over my womb, and she never experienced feeling Nova's kicks as I always envisioned. Still to this day thinking of this shatters my heart.

Our in-person baby shower got canceled. We ended up having it as a virtual one, hosted through a virtual venue from the loneliness of our humble home. There were no hugs or group photos with our family and friends in front of a beautiful background surrounded by all the presents and baby decorations. It was only me in the baby shower pictures. I was wearing a beautiful white gown and a flower crown, and I was standing in front of the mailed-in gifts behind me, instead of standing next to my family and friends.

Any in-person prenatal Yoga sessions or birthing-related classes we had booked were also canceled. Doctor visits changed. Husbands were no longer allowed inside the doctor's office with the mother-to-be. Jeremy missed the last few ultrasounds, and I had to make any decisions on my own while being checked by the doctor, and handle any good or bad news on my own moving forward. Inside those doctor appointments, there was no one to hold my hand if needed.

After halfway through my pregnancy doctors canceled all the in-person prenatal checks too. Everything was online-only, and I had to buy a Baby Doppler to monitor my baby's heartbeat on my own, and a blood pressure cuff to monitor my levels at home. Complete insanity.

In the midst of it all, feeling Nova inside me kept me going. I fixed my eyes on Jesus and the prize: my baby. My love for her gave me a sense of inner peace, and somehow it helped me to oversee all the bad things happening around the world.

My pregnancy saved me from it all, it was a shield made of light glowing around me. It transformed me and strengthened me.

> **Pregnancy is a miracle; it creates a baby, and at the same time it creates a mother in the most extraordinary way.**

Darkest Before Dawn

Close to my due date, hospital rules changed drastically. Doulas were no longer allowed in the hospital to assist us during labor as we originally planned. Some hospitals in many cities went even further and didn't allow husbands to be with the mother in labor as their support person.

Mothers around the globe were bringing babies to this world without their partners, family members, friends, or doulas; without those they fully trusted. Laboring mothers could only count on the limited help nurses and doctors were able to provide, their overall availability, and the number of patients they were taking care of at the same time. In my opinion—and from my own experience—it was inhuman, inconsiderate, and unfair.

What a crazy time to be pregnant for the very first time in your life. My faith was shaken.

As my due date was approaching, I felt terrified of the possibility of not being able to have Jeremy by my side during labor. I felt I could handle anything but that. Everything was on the line and subject to last-minute changes with hospitals. We were at the mercy of these institutions and their rules, and there was nothing we could do about it. I had to let go, surrender to my human limitations, and give up control—because, in reality, it was all out of my control—and I needed to let God take the wheel. What a humbling experience. I got on my knees and I prayed.

Jeremy was allowed in the hospital room with me when I was in labor—which was not the case for many of my friends who delivered babies around the same time in other states and countries. As much as I was thankful for it, it was literally just myself and Jeremy to get through it all. No doula, no family members, or close friends were allowed with us as they would normally do in the past.

This is not how we planned things at all.

> **The truth is, you can plan a day in your head a thousand times and it can still go very differently from how you originally imagined it.**

The same can be said on the day Nova was born.

When I was 40 weeks pregnant, my ultrasound showed my amniotic fluid was low, and they told me I needed to be induced right away. I asked for alternatives but they gave me none. According to them, there was nothing else they could do and my baby needed to be born that day. I found out later how their statement was not entirely true, she didn't *have* to be born that same day, and there were options, but those options were not offered to me at the time, especially because of COVID restrictions.

Basically, they told me I had to leave the doctor's office, go home, pick up our bags, and go back to the hospital to be admitted and start the process. I wasn't able to get a second opinion. I tried to reach out to other practices and doctors, but no one picked up the phone. I felt so hopeless and voiceless.

Jeremy was waiting for me outside in the car because husbands were not allowed inside the medical offices, and my cellphone's signal was extremely weak, so I wasn't able to talk to him or anyone on the phone until I was dispatched and I got out of the doctor's office. The minutes I waited to be out and finally talk to him felt like an eternity.

We prayed together in the car and cried our hearts out asking God for direction and strength. We went home, finished packing our bags, and off we went to deliver our baby under the most strange and authoritarian regime I've personally ever experienced in my history with hospitals.

We couldn't get inside the hospital without a mask on, they would take our body temperature and ask us a bunch of questions about if we were recently exposed to COVID, and then everyone needed to keep what they called a "social distance" from anyone else, at least six feet apart from each other.

When we got inside our room, I noticed it had a big nice tub. I felt so happy thinking maybe I was going to be able to submerge myself in the water while in labor, to help me ease the contraction pains. I thought there was still hope for me to avoid an epidural entirely. Little did I know that from the very beginning, I was going to experience a chain of interventions, and still to date I regret allowing them.

> **Laboring took me to the bottom of myself. I endured unspeakable things, and still today I can't explain how I was able to handle them but only by the grace of God.**

I remember I was even asked by a nurse to put on a face mask while I was unsuccessfully pushing my baby out—which lasted about four hours—even though my COVID test from when I was admitted to the hospital was negative. Imagine that for a second. It was madness! The abuse of power being hammered down on laboring mothers during those days was outrageous.

I was induced on Friday evening, and I delivered my baby via an unplanned C-Section the following Monday. It's interesting to think that I was told Nova needed to be born on Friday, but she was born perfectly fine four days later.

Even though I was deeply thankful and relieved that she was complete and healthy, I mourned my hopes for a natural labor and birth experience greatly.

The Creation of a Star

Nova was born on June 15, 2020, and that day a new Gloria was born with her. Nothing has transformed me as a woman—and as a leader—as much as becoming a mother.

Babies are light in its purest form, bright enough to make a glare in the darkest of circumstances. Nova is the perfect example of it.

The first time I ever held her in my arms, it was as if my heart was going to explode out of my chest. I'm pretty sure my level of oxytocin hormones skyrocketed! I looked down at her beautiful tiny face, and I realized I created her. MY BODY created a human being! What a badass woman I was!

I felt honored that God allowed me to bring a life into this world, and I was experiencing for the first time the most utterly, reckless, and overwhelming love. I knew I wanted nothing more than to shower Nova with warmth and affection for the rest of my life. I wanted her to have the knowledge to pursue anything her heart desired, and for her to grow up knowing that as a woman there were no limits to her dreams. She was perfect, loved, and mine.

Instantly, I cared for her and loved her more than anything else in the world. Everything else became background noise, a sound in the distance.

> **Even though motherhood is a high-pressure job—it can be challenging, scary, unpredictable, and chaotic—it's the most empowering and fulfilling of them all.**

I love you, my precious little girl. I will always do everything in my power to help you reach your dreams—I whispered while my heart was bursting at her bare sight.

Even though things didn't end up being at all how I pictured them initially, I was grateful Jeremy was there with me to support me through it all, and to witness the birth of our little miracle. Despite everything happening in the world, Nova was the light that shone in the darkness and chased away the shadows.

YOUR TURN:

1. Have you ever mourned an experience you planned with so much love and enthusiasm, but the outcome was completely different from what you envisioned?

   _____

   _____

2. When have you felt relieved by letting go of the weight of trying to keep things together, and accepting it's out of your control?

   _____

   _____

3. When have you come back stronger after going through a very difficult experience?

   _____

   _____

4. Can a baby be the light in the middle of the darkness?

   _____

   _____

TAKEAWAYS:

- Pregnancy is a glowing shield.
- It's ok to plan things out, like your pregnancy and labor experiences, and it's also ok mourning if they turn out to be different from what you expected.
- Mourning your birth experience while having a perfect and healthy baby, doesn't make you a bad mom.
- Your feelings and hopes matter.
- Babies are glowing lights.

Draw Your Thoughts

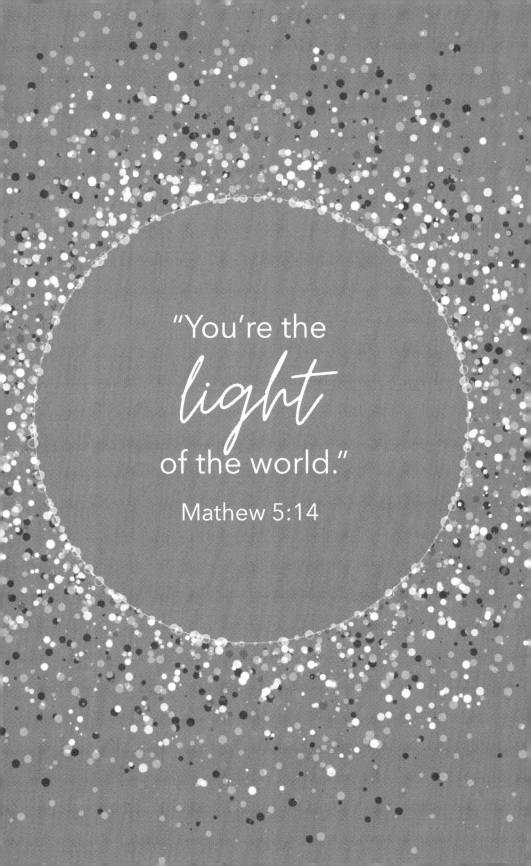

Chapter 4

Trailblazing Calling

Time won't stop waiting for us, and this fact might make us feel like we must keep moving at all costs. We all learn and build up from different experiences in life, good and bad, but what if at some point we realize we're not walking in the right direction? What if we aren't where we are supposed to be?

> **Sometimes we need to slow down and take a break in order to hear from God and reassess our purpose in life.**

I agree it's important to keep taking one step after the other to accomplish things in life, as long as it's on the correct path that will ultimately help you reach the bigger calling we all have in this world.

The Fourth Trimester

After Nova was born, the work I had to do in the first 8-12 weeks of her life was no joke. There are no words, no books, and no documentary, nothing that could have possibly prepared me in full for the first few weeks of motherhood. I believe everyone has to live it in the flesh and experience it in their own way to truly understand the struggles, and the outstanding amount of love your heart is capable of giving.

Based on my own experience, the first days with my newborn were the most chaotic, yet the most precious ones. It's such a unique time in life and—as everyone will tell you—those first few days go by so fast. If you're a new mom, make sure to slow down, soak it all in, and enjoy it to the fullest while it lasts.

My priorities overall shifted entirely since her arrival, and during the first few weeks, I was completely focused on taking care of Nova and myself. I was learning how to breastfeed her, healing my body—both physically and mentally—and navigating this whole new world that motherhood was for me.

Breastfeeding alone comes with great work and sacrifice; if anyone ever tells you that one of the advantages of breastfeeding is that it is *free* they don't know the value of a woman's time and effort.

I spent countless hours each day and night liquefying myself to feed my little milkaholic baby. Yet, as hard as it was, I wouldn't change it for the world.

> **Nothing can be compared to the connection a woman has with her baby while they are breastfeeding. It's sacred.**

I understand that not every woman wants to breastfeed—it's a very personal choice—but I chose to do it because after lots of research about its benefits, I was certain it was the best for my baby. Though, it wasn't easy. In fact, breastfeeding was one of the biggest challenges I've faced as a new mother—more on that later.

When Nova and I were able to overcome all of our initial breastfeeding challenges, and things were finally working how they were supposed to in that matter, breastfeeding was one of the best experiences I've ever had in my life. I treasure the memories of it greatly. If you're a mother-to-be—or a brand new mom—I pray you're able to experience it too, if that's something your heart desires.

The journey may not be easy, but it's worth it.

Sleep deprivation is real. There were many sleepless nights—even though Nova slept long hours from early on—in my case, my lack of sleep was related to the breastfeeding issues. I was dealing with a low milk supply, so I had to get up every two hours to breast pump myself until my milk supply was fixed.

Sometimes Nova would also fight her sleep, and it was challenging to help her fall asleep peacefully.

Between the sleepless nights due to milk pumping, and her struggles to fall asleep, it did begin to weigh on me, and at some point, I started feeling tired all-the-time.

I heard so many times the tale of how breastfeeding is also great for the mother because it will help you lose your pregnancy weight right away. That was not the case for me, it was quite the opposite.

I also developed diastasis recti, a condition that some women experience after birth when the abdominal muscles are separated due to excessive stretching of the connective tissue.

My list of challenges could go on and on. The beauty behind this series of unfortunate events is that for every problem, I came up with a new solution, and from every obstacle, I came out of it wiser, stronger, and more confident as a mother.

> "And we know that in all things God works for the good of those who love him, who have been called according to his purpose." Romans 8:28

The struggles a new mom faces can feel never-ending, and sometimes these difficulties will overlap with each other. Trouble will appear out of thin air and you may not get a break in between. In the midst of things, just remember to trust your maternal instinct. You can do this. This is why it is so important to take those first few months to focus on you and your baby. This intimate time with Nova is what worked best for me. Eventually, everything fell into place as I mastered my motherhood ninja skills.

In contrast to all the challenges, motherhood also brings—on a daily basis—an overwhelming amount of joy. Some of the memories I cherish the most are related to witnessing Nova's firsts. The first time she held her head up, the first time she smiled, the first time she giggled, the first time she said 'Mama'—I even got to record on video the first time she rolled over! It was all so exciting!

Ironically with every first, there's also a last. Sometimes these changes happen so fast we don't get a chance to say goodbye to the previous chapters. I remember the day when Nova's first two bottom teeth came through her gums. I was so thrilled! Yet, with a pang, I realized I was no longer going to see her beautiful toothless smile anymore.

The fourth trimester looks different for everyone. For some, it can be easier, for others it will be harder. It was very hard on me. Just know this is a precious and priceless time, and it will not last forever. Keep your eyes on the prize: your well-being and your baby's. Everything else can wait until you're ready for it.

Transitioning Into Reality

As time began to pass by, Jeremy and I began to conquer our new life as parents. Slowly, I was able to settle some things and dedicate time again to my professional career goals, which I had put on hold during the first few months of Nova's life.

My main concern was figuring out how I was going to be the mother and architect I always envisioned to be; someone who was actively involved and present in my child's life, but also an architect that would make a positive impact on the profession of architecture, and to the lives of those I served. These roles were both equally important to me.

Having a child is a huge responsibility.

> **Selflessness is prevalent in motherhood, and more often than not, mothers feel pressured to give up their careers and even give up on themselves.**

Who they truly were as individuals can disappear, as they sacrifice everything for the sake of their children.

They say you end up coming second because your child will always come first. And even though there is truth in this statement, I felt it shouldn't be so black and white when we add our professional life into the equation.

> **Women have been the backbone of the nuclear family for a very long time.**

Women have been the backbone of the nuclear family for a very long time, and those who are in the field of business, paving their way in the world, are battling on a daily basis trying to find a balance between their roles as mothers and as professionals. Flexibility in the work environment is one of the things most industries—but especially architecture—lack the most.

This can make us see motherhood as a terrifying prospect in a great deal of ways. It's hard going against the common mindset. I know it was hard for me, but I always thought there should be a way to balance things out. Sometimes it feels like a rite of passage in a way that once you become a mother, you may also give up on your career.

I always disagreed with that perspective and the burden that is commonly put on mothers. In my opinion, that theory was missing an essential piece of the puzzle.

As human beings, we need to understand our purpose in life, our true calling. To some women, their purpose in life **IS** to have children, and by doing so they feel fulfilled, accomplished, and completed in life. And believe me, those are hardworking women as well. To some women, their calling is completely focused on their careers, and they pour their hearts and souls into serving their professions. Then, to some of us, our purpose in life involves motherhood tied up together with other things.

Because of my faith, I've learned throughout the years that our identity is in Christ, and we need to embrace who we are in Him to thrive. If we don't, we're not able to achieve our own definition of happiness and success, with or without children.

My biggest question at this point was: *what is my true calling in life? What did God want me to do moving forward?*

After a lot of thought and prayer, I realized that even if I didn't believe what that lady told me back in 2009, about what God had in store for me, it didn't matter. He truly had bigger plans for me, and one by one they became true. Yes, those plans involved motherhood, but they also involved other aspects of my life and my professional career. It didn't end with Nova.

Back to Business

As my maternity leave was coming to an end around September 2020, Jeremy and I started making plans of how I was going to incorporate myself back into my old job and how we were going to handle things with Nova. In the middle of this process, I felt a sense of sadness that I couldn't quite explain. I realized the thought of going back to work made me unhappy, but what I found interesting was that it wasn't about me not letting go of Nova or mourning the fact that I was not going to be around her 24/7 anymore. This sorrow came from a different place in my heart.

After almost two years of making excuses, it finally reached me and hit me like a wrecking ball.

I was disappointed in myself.

Don't get me wrong, I was thankful for the opportunities I had through my previous employer. They allowed me to provide for my family when we needed it the most, and I gained valuable experience from my years working for them. I also met some of the most wonderful people in this industry through them, with some of them being my best friends now.

> **But it was no secret that I always dreamed of having an architecture studio that I could call my own.**

It was never my vision to grow in the corporate world and work for someone else forever. This was supposed to be a transitional phase in my life, a necessary evil. The only reason I took a job in the USA was that I had to in order to complete the process to transfer my architecture license to Florida. I couldn't practice architecture independently without that license.

Yet, that process was already in the past. I have had my architecture license in the United States since early 2019. What was my excuse at this point? Why was I no longer pursuing the one dream that kept me motivated and helped me to move forward through that long and grueling licensing process?

Why had I put my dreams on hold? I love my daughter, but this had nothing to do with my role as her mother. I wasn't giving up my career, I was going back to work! But going back to my job didn't reflect the direction I wanted to take for my professional future. I wasn't walking toward the path leading me to my definition of success, and deep inside I knew it. I was torn.

It felt like I had suddenly settled for something different from what I wanted for myself. I had the connections, the support from my husband, the experience, and the skills to create my studio, yet I wasn't making the move. But why? Why had my career come to a grinding halt?

Fear.

There. I said it. That was my answer. I was fearful of the unknown, of having our financial stability at risk, but most of all, I was afraid I was going to become a failure in the eyes of those around me.

My job was safe, and any decision that I made moving forward was no longer just about me. Things had drastically changed; it was now about what was best for all of us, but most importantly, what was best for Nova.

I felt fear, and I had no idea how to overcome it.

Do you fear yourself? Fear to take a step forward to accomplish that one big dream and then fail? Fear of not being good enough?

Fear is a taskmaster.

> **Fear can control us if we let it, and fear of failure is far worse than fear itself.**

Fear will paralyze us completely—and in order to overcome it, one needs to start by understanding what fear is, where it comes from, face it and take steps of faith to move forward.

So what is fear after all? The Merriam-Webster Dictionary defines it as "an unpleasant often strong emotion caused by anticipation or awareness of danger." [1] This perception can be real as well as imagined. This last part struck me, it was quite revealing and liberating.

Did my fear have grounds to withstand and govern my decisions, or was it all in my head?

One of the things that helped me the most to answer this fundamental question and conquer my own fear, was asking myself what was the worst thing that could happen if I would fail and then imagining how I could solve each scenario if, in the end, the worst was the outcome of my crazy adventure.

To me, the worst that could happen if I would fail was having to go back to a job. But see… that wasn't so bad after all. I was also terrified of failing as a mother. Yet, reflecting on this made me realize there was no room for failure in the equation, in motherhood failure was not an option.

I needed to find a balance between my career and my family, and I wanted to own my architectural business again. I owed that much to myself. I worked hard for it and I needed to take a leap of faith… even if I had to do it afraid.

It starts with me igniting the fire within. It starts by trusting in God's plan and in myself. It starts with taking one single step forward.

And the Glow Shall Set You Free

I know God's timing is perfect, so I decided to wait on Him first. During the next couple of weeks, night after night, I prayed about it with my husband. We wanted to hear from God. We asked for wisdom and discernment, and we wanted to have the reassurance that any direction we would choose, it was the one He wanted for us to take.

And one day, I woke up early in the morning, and as I was doing my devotional, I read these verses in the Bible:

> "You are the light of the world.

A town built on a hill cannot be hidden. Neither do people light a lamp and put it under a bowl. Instead, they put it on its stand, and it gives light to everyone in the house. In the same way, let your light shine before others, that they may see your good deeds and glorify your Father in Heaven," Mathew 5:14-16.

Instantly I felt that inner peace that can only be felt when God speaks to you through the Holy Spirit. I knew it in my heart at that moment, God wanted me to be a light in the life of others, and I was ready for the task. I held faith that everything was going to work out in the end—and that all I needed to do was take a step forward in the direction He was guiding me to.

I decided to quit my job—September 29 was my last day working for them—and Glow Architects was born.

It's funny in a way, glow used to be my nickname when I was back in architecture school. It all came like a shooting star into my life. Everything seemed to slide into place from that point on, and I knew exactly where I was heading.

I set to work, and some people did not hold their tongues about my choices. They made me feel like I was crazy for quitting my job and creating a new architecture studio in Florida, while I was still a new mother and a so-called pandemic was still running rampant around the world.

Many people around me thought it was a terrible idea and that I was jeopardizing my family. Many people criticized me directly and indirectly for what I was doing at the time.

This may have happened to you at some point in your life, feeling lots of pressure from other people's opinions. Maybe you lived it in a similar scenario or maybe it's in a completely different story. It doesn't matter. You just need to remember that when someone tells you something is impossible to do, their opinion is based on their own limitations. Their reality doesn't need to be yours. God has the last word, always, and sometimes we need to shut our ears from the noise around us, in order to hear from Him clearly.

> **When someone tells you something is impossible to do, their opinion is based on their own limitations. Their reality doesn't need to be yours.**

Of course, there was one more detail people focused on and felt that I was being irresponsible for not taking into consideration. Our country's economy was being horribly impacted as a result of the pandemic, presidential elections were around the corner, no one knew what was going to happen, and people everywhere were losing jobs every single day. So many people thought of me as insane for quitting a stable job, and to attempt starting a business in the midst of it all.

Ironically, the darkness surrounding the world at the moment didn't discourage me. Quite the opposite, it motivated me because I was so certain this was my calling. God told me I was meant to bring light to the world and shine before others. There was no turning back. I was armored with a shield of faith, committed to demystifying the glowing balance between motherhood and business- and from that, so could any other woman.

YOUR TURN:

1. What unfortunate event have you gone through that made you stronger afterward?
   _____
   _____

2. What are your purpose and true calling in life?
   _____
   _____

3. When was the last time fear stopped you from doing something you wanted?
   _____
   _____

4. What is the worst that can happen if things don't turn out as you envisioned?
   _____
   _____

TAKEAWAYS:

- Motherhood is not easy, but it sure is the most fulfilling journey of them all.
- Every obstacle in life brings an opportunity to learn and grow.
- Your calling doesn't need to be limited to only one thing in life.
- If you can handle the worst, fear can't control you.
- You're meant for something bigger than you may understand. Let God guide you through His divine plan.

Draw Your Thoughts

"No other business in life is as challenging and *rewarding* as the business of motherhood."

Gloria Kloter

Chapter 5

Owning a Business

One myth I had feared to be true for so long was that motherhood and professional success did not entwine.

Architecture—like many other careers—is still a male-dominated profession. According to the American Institute of Architects (AIA), 2020 Membership Demographics Report, only 1.85% of their registered architect members are Latinas.[1] How could I contribute and make a difference to uplift others around me? I felt Glow Architects was the answer.

Starting and running your own company can feel like a big and overwhelming puzzle. Just like in motherhood, entrepreneurship comes with its own challenges and many unknowns. Even if you think you had it all figured out before you start—like I mistakenly thought—you'll continuously find new hurdles to overcome throughout your journey.

If you feel this chapter is not for you because your business may not be related to architecture, or if owning a business isn't something you've ever considered as part of your professional plan, please bear with me. My intention is not to become the next business guru on how to run a successful business, but to share useful knowledge that I have acquired through my own experience, and share insights that could add value to your career path and spark a different mindset in you.

See, motherhood taught me more about managing a business than I initially realized. It might do—or has done already—the same for you.

> **No other business in life is as challenging and rewarding as the business of motherhood.**

If you can be a mother, you can most definitely master business ownership. The beauty of it all is you get to create your own vision of things and bless others while you're at it.

Nobody Said It Was Easy

Establishing a business while raising a child is quite a daunting task. I always joke that I had "pandemic twins" as I ended up having a baby and starting a business at the same time. I officially launched Glow Architects in October 2020, not too long after I quit my previous job, and Nova was barely four months old.

Both the business and caring for my baby took so much out of me mentally and physically, but the more I dug deeper into mastering motherhood, the more I realized the similarities it had with my career and how the skills I was developing as a mother were essential to managing my business too.

This realization helped me to put a set system in place to manage both parts of my life effectively. The new level of awareness, organization, discipline, resiliency, and selfless leadership continuously growing inside of me played an important role in how I was able to handle the difficulties I encountered when I started my business in America. I don't think I would have survived without it!

The truth is, it was quite strange following this process in this country. There were many differences between how I did things back in the Dominican Republic and how I had to do it in the US. To give you some quick examples, establishing an entity in my home country was simpler, the level of liability for architects was lower, the materials and systems commonly used there were my bread and butter, and I was speaking in my first language. These conditions allowed me to take bolder steps early in my career and even get heavily involved in areas I wouldn't get involved here, like acting as the general contractor for some of my projects. The simplicity of things back there—in comparison to how things work here—is part of the reason why I managed to thrive there so rapidly and at such a young age.

The opposite can be said of my experience in this country. I had to re-learn many steps in a secondary language, and regulations were way more complicated than what I was used to. I had to put my creative self on the side to let my analytical self help me to figure things out.

I think it's fair to say the amount of paperwork and details you need to think about and take care of can be overwhelming, especially because some of those I had to learn and figure out on my own.

It was funny in a way, I felt like I was going through the motions of motherhood all over again—creating something from nothing.

Some of the things I had to do were:
- Choose a name
- Design a logo
- Establish an LLC
- Work on the businesses core values
- Learn the intricacies of taxes
- Understand and get all the different insurances needed
- Purchase equipment
- Purchase furniture
- Buy and install computer software
- Create templates
- Build a website
- Design business cards
- Work on marketing pieces
- Manage contracts
- Manage risks
- Manage liabilities
- And so much more…

With everything I completed, there were always at least ten other things to learn or do.

A person could always pay for other professionals to take care of some of these initial tasks, but I didn't have the capital to spend, and for that reason, I had to do most of it myself. This business was my brainchild and I was putting in the work and doing everything in my power to make it a successful one.

Thinking outside of the box was part of my strategy. At the time I started my business, I didn't have enough savings yet to rent or buy a place for my studio. So I worked from home at first and offered alternative solutions to meet with clients—like meeting them in their own office, or taking them out for lunch or a coffee—I did what I could with what I had at the moment. Eventually, I was able to have my own space. I cherish the memory of the day when we installed the plaque with the company's name and logo next to the entrance door. This small detail made it all feel real. I was happy to slowly be gaining control over my professional life again.

It's Not Only What You Know, but Who You Know

If I could travel in time and give my young self a single piece of advice it would be:

> "You don't need to know it all, what you need to know is where to find the answers to the things you don't."

I think anyone who is trying to build a new business should find a business coach to help them navigate different areas of their business. At a minimum, I would recommend having a person (or a support group) who helps you organize your ideas and sets milestones with you. This will give you a sense of accountability and assist you in working harder towards your goals.

In addition, you should have mentors—close friends, and other business owners from your community—the more mentors the better. No one is an expert on everything, so you want to be able to ask different people about different things, depending on where their experience and expertise lie.

It's important to have people to fall back on and speak to about the things you're unsure of. This in turn will help you grow your business and manage it better.

Use the resources available to you, the people within your community are your tribe. Pick up the phone and ask them questions. Believe it or not, some of them will be learning with—and from—you. Eventually, some of these colleagues and mentors of yours will also become referral partners for you—and you for them—as they'll get projects their way that won't fit their business model but may fit yours, and vice versa.

For some, finding a mentor or a support group could be difficult, so one way I personally found help was by getting involved in some of the online communities related to my industry, which are available through different social media platforms.

Some of the online support groups on platforms like Facebook that I'm currently a part of (but not limited to) are:

- Foreign Architects
- Parents in Architecture
- The Launching & Evolving Architectural Practice (LEAP) Group
- The ARE Facebook Group
- Women Architects Collective
- Next Architects Community
- The Entre-Architect Community

Hundreds of people share their knowledge and help each other without spending a penny. This can be a great way to build new relationships with like-minded individuals. As we plunge further into the digital age, it's easier than ever to connect with others—so you might as well take advantage of it.

I reached out to people in my region and others from different states. I asked questions about their design services, their business structure, and any examples or templates they could share with me for documents, requirements, and policies that I needed to put into place for my own company. It was most helpful and quite enlightening.

> **I learned in this process how open and transparent people can be in sharing details of their business when you ask with humbleness and express your genuine desire to learn from them.**

Based on my experience, prepare yourself for an overwhelming amount of information that you may not be able to handle all at once.

I also learned that in America people can operate their businesses very differently from each other, and still be successful in their own way. There is no one-size-fits-all approach to doing things. What may work for someone else, might not work for you, but there are always golden nuggets that can make all the difference for you. Keep paying attention to what others do and say, and try to implement things as you go, until you figure out what works best for you and your business.

It's important to learn from others while creating your own way of doing things, and sometimes this process implies making mistakes along the way. We just need to be open and embrace those errors, implement new strategies, and keep moving forward.

Your Business Plan to Plan Your Business

Have you ever heard of a business plan or why you should have one for your business? A business plan in itself is basically a set of steps designed to help you succeed.

Overall, the business plan is like the guidebook of your business; it explains what it does, what your expected profits are, why people need it, why you want to do the business, your assets, how much people might need to invest in it—it basically has EVERYTHING.

On paper it sounds easy enough, right? But in reality, it takes a great deal of time and dedication to create one properly.

> **Having a business plan from the beginning will help you stay focused on the specific tasks you need to succeed and accomplish short-term and long-term goals.**

This piece is especially important if you envision bringing in any investors or to use any lenders in the future.

There are many different ways to create your business plan, but here is a basic outline of where to start:

1. An overview of the company
2. A brief description of the business
3. A market analysis
4. A comprehensive operating plan
5. A strategic marketing and sales plan
6. A financial plan

Working on your business plan can help you get started on estimating your start-up costs, and profit and loss projections. These types of tasks are important to do correctly from the beginning, and having a business coach can be a tool and great help to wrap your head around it. Get one if you can.

Your Network Is Your Net Worth

After completing some of the initial steps to launching, it was a matter of setting the wheels in motion to get my clients. A good friend of mine—who is an interior designer, mother, and business owner—told me once, "Gloria, be mentally ready to put on the work. As soon as you start telling people that you're opening your business, they will throw business opportunities your way, probably more than what you'll be able to handle." She was right.

Personally, I was lucky to have built a great personal and professional network during my time in the United States, especially through the wonderful community I found inside the Young Architect's ARE Boot Camp by my mentor and friend, Michael Riscica. This program is dedicated to mentoring the next generation of architects where licensing candidates from all over the United States work together towards this common goal, but it goes beyond that. I took the ARE Bootcamp when I was studying for the architect registration examination (ARE), but I stayed around as part of the Young Architect family afterward, and through it, I met some of my best friends and mentors.

I also developed my network when I served in different local and national organizations related to the architecture field.

> **The wonderful people I met through these experiences were my rock and they guided me through my journey as a new business owner.**

The strongest client relationships I ended up developing, however, were through the local Real Estate Investors Association (REIA), which is a community of local investors. These investors were constantly building, renovating, and acquiring new residential and commercial properties for business purposes.

Whether you're planning to start a business or not, it's important to connect with local associations related to your career, and also those who are part of the sphere of influence within your industry.

A couple of good examples of this for those who are in the AEC (Architecture, Engineering, and Construction) industry are the local chapters of institutions like the American Institute of Architects (AIA), Commercial Real Estate Women (CREW), National Association of Women in Construction (NAWIC), the Chambers of Commerce, and others. A good way to find other organizations and events is through meetup.com.

As a woman in business—whether you're a business owner or not—my advice would be to consistently attend the meetings held by the local chapters of the institutions related to your career. Do some research and identify what's available in your area and take a look at their event's calendar.

Networking this way is how I met most of my current clients and referral partners, including general contractors, engineers, and developers. I attended as many meetings as I could and networked with them way before I started my business.

This in turn developed long-lasting relationships, and through that my business blossomed further. You need people to help you grow and without them, you will find it ten times harder to succeed.

> Successful businesses are built through strong relationships.

Volunteering is an Investment

Another way to increase both your network and connections is by volunteering, and therefore, giving back to your community. Have you ever heard of that old saying, "People don't care how much you know until they know how much you care," by Theodore Roosevelt? This concept has a great deal of merit to it.

When you volunteer your time and expertise to help others, you can potentially become a leader to them. To be a great leader, you have to genuinely care for others, their career, aspirations, and even their personal lives. Caring for other people will in turn make them care about you. Compassion creates more compassion, and if there's anything we need more of in this world, it is most definitely that!

One of the awards I've been honored with throughout my career, is the Kelley Emerging Professional Award 2020, which I received from the American Institute of Architects of Tampa Bay in 2020.[2] I was awarded it due to how much I'd given to our community and the number of people I've helped throughout my own journey. In particular, I used my own experience to help others who were in a similar situation to mine, assisting foreign architects and professionals who were trying to become registered architects in the US.

The need to help these individuals came from my heart and I never made any money out of it. It was my way of giving back. I saw that other people were stuck on the same path I was before I established my firm, and I knew I should make myself available to serve as a guide and provide a network for them where they could feel safe, talk about their experiences, and seek help when needed.

It can be so hard when you're knowledgeable and experienced about a subject, but for whatever circumstances in your life, you end up moving to a place or country where your knowledge is not recognized or your expertise is still not relevant or valued. I lived it in the flesh, and I know how lonely and hopeless one can feel. That's how the Foreign Architects private community on Facebook was founded, where I mentor many others free of charge and continue to do so.

I never expected to receive an award for my efforts, but it's an honor I'll never take for granted. When you invest in others you're also investing in yourself.

Designing the Trust You Can Build Upon

> **People do business with those they know, like, and trust.**

I think it would be very hard for anyone to build up a business without developing credibility in the marketplace. Would you trust someone who you had never met, or that no one else around you had heard of before?

People naturally want to be around those that they can trust, not around those they feel are only after getting business from them. Instead, people want to work with those they consider qualified, professional, and most importantly, trustworthy.

Many of my clients have become repeat clients with multiple projects that we've helped them with, which in turn has also created a long-term friendship between us. I personally believe this speaks louder than anything else about my work ethic and professionalism.

It's important that people can put their trust in me to transform their vision into buildings and spaces to inhabit.

> **Any architectural project represents an investment for every client, and there are a lot of financial and emotional factors involved.**

I knew that besides being competent and talented, having a sense of connection and community with my clients was one of the most important things to accomplish.

If you're wondering how you could make a lasting impression with your clients too, my simple answer is you need to let people see you as a friendly and an approachable human being who happens to be an expert in a specific field or trade they need services from—all the things which your business should strive to be. Allow them to relate to you.

Know Your Worth

Initially, one particular thing I struggled with was understanding how to properly charge for my professional services. This might happen in many other career fields, but in architecture, it was hard to discover accurate information and comparable data on how to charge my clients for my architectural and design services. This made it difficult at times to understand what direction was the best to take whenever new leads and potential clients would reach out asking for design fee proposals for their projects.

How to bill for your services is an unspoken topic in general. After getting burned once or twice, I learned my lesson. It wasn't until I spoke directly and openly with a couple of colleagues and mentors that I started to figure this out.

On the first few projects I got under contract, I aimed to calculate the number of hours it would take me to do a specific project, and based on those expected hours of production, I would calculate my design fee, but almost every time I ended up undercharging. Things always looked very simple at the beginning, but then unforeseen challenges would creep in.

I must admit another mistake on my part was not asking enough questions during my initial consultation meetings with the clients. I was so eager to start working on my own projects again, I jumped too soon into a couple of them which ended up being way harder than I anticipated.

Another challenge in calculating my fees, was that not every project would fit within the profit model based on a percentage of the construction budget, or a multiplier of the total square footage of the project. Sometimes the scenarios were not as simple to fit in a specific box alone.

In the end, what worked best for us was doing a spreadsheet with a combination of all the different ways one can calculate a design fee. We would play around with the multipliers and percentages from one system to another, and make our best judgment based on a couple of factors. Some of the things we started taking into account (but not limited to) were:

- The level of experience of the client with construction timelines and processes.
- The specific type of project they were hiring us for.
- The team involved with the client—if there was an owner's representative or a general contractor acting as a project manager.
- The stakeholders involved and how this could affect the decision-making process—including any other owners that needed to be a part of the contract, historical review boards, HOA, and others.
- The specifics related to the county we were going to deal with for permitting, as we discovered the hard way how the level of requirements could vary greatly from one county to another, and sometimes these differences added complexity and extra time to our permitting process significantly.
- If this was a one-time client versus a repeat client.

Most importantly, after figuring out where we needed to be price-wise, we also learned a very important piece of the puzzle, which is explaining to our clients the value we bring to the table as a company, and the reason why our services had that cost for that specific project.

Not everyone was willing to pay for it, and that's ok. You can be open and have a small room for negotiation if needed, but it's up to a limit.

Know your worth and stick to it.

You don't want to get stuck with a contract in which the fee doesn't make sense for your company's model and internal expenses. Sometimes you win by letting go of things that are just not a good fit for you.

The Ideal Client

Every business has an ideal client, and that's the one they will most likely focus on targeting in any marketing campaign or business generation strategy. Sometimes when we're starting a business, we might think we're sure of who we want to work with and the type of projects we'll focus on, but as you experience different scenarios your mindset in this matter might vary. This was the case for me.

Surprisingly, my ideal client wasn't exactly who I originally thought it was going to be. The more I worked with different people and projects, the more I learned about myself and where I needed to be. The things I knew and liked to work with from my experience in the Dominican Republic didn't necessarily apply to my experience in the USA.

I rediscovered myself as a business owner in this country. Most of my residential clients are not the end-users or final owners of the projects I'm designing. The end-users were the vast majority of my clients in the Dominican and, together with some other specific criteria, they were my ideal client back there. I thought this was going to be the case here too, but I was wrong.

Instead, we're working with investors, developers, and general contractors as primary residential clients, and some of them also generate leads for us. Most of them are building-to-sell, not to keep or live in. We don't do many residential remodeling jobs anymore, instead, we're focused on new builds. This is different for our commercial clients where we take on both renovations and ground-up projects, and in general, that's what works best for our business.

Remember Your *Why*

Setting up the business, just like the first couple of months of being a mother, was incredibly taxing and tiring. Something important to think about whenever you find yourself struggling in your business journey is your *why*—which many people do not reflect on as much when they face challenges and feel discouraged.

My *why* was defined from early on: I wanted to find a balance between architecture and motherhood without compromising either role.

> **I wanted to put an end to the expectation that women can't be in business and raise a family while being successful at both.**

I knew I wanted to do this for myself and for other women in business, but I also wanted to do it for my daughter.

Whenever I felt like quitting it all, I circled back to my why and it helped me to push through it.

Define Success

People believe success is defined by leaps and bounds, but the only definition of success that truly matters is the one that you set for yourself.

To me, success meant glowing as a business owner and as a mom while fulfilling my calling in life in alignment with God's purpose.

> **Being a mother and an architect shaped the path of how I wanted to live my life and the things that made me truly happy. Nova made me happy.**

Creating my own business made me happy. Both gave me plenty of challenges, and at the same time, both journeys offered me unlimited possibilities and the flexibility to change my direction and my approach to things as needed. I was in charge and the balance I had established allowed me to thrive.

Success is different for everyone—each person can have a unique definition of what success should be. Define yours.

What makes YOU happy? What do YOU enjoy? Where do you see YOUR LIFE going? What do YOU want to accomplish? What do YOU want to be remembered for? These are questions only you can answer.

Nobody else's opinions matter on this. *Never* let what other people think define where your journey goes. Only God and you alone can choose the finish line. Don't let others' limitations limit you as well.

Seek God's guidance and clarity about His plans for you and your purpose in life. He will answer and help you achieve your own success, however it may be defined in your heart.

YOUR TURN:

1. Who is in your professional circle that can be a mentor to you?
   _____
   _____

2. Which professional communities in your area could you get involved with this week?
   _____
   _____

3. How can you give back to your community?
   _____
   _____

4. How do you define success?
   _____
   _____

TAKEAWAYS:

- Motherhood can be your best and biggest mentor.
- Get involved within your community, remember giving is receiving.
- Your ideal client can evolve over time.
- Your why is your anchor.
- Your definition of success is unique and it's the only one that matters.

Draw Your Thoughts

"Architecture is an interdisciplinary, *collaborative,* and creative world. The same can be said for motherhood."

Gloria Kloter

Chapter 6

Grow Your Support System

"For just as each of us has one body with many members, and these members do not all have the same function, so in Christ we, though many, form one body, and each member belongs to all the others." Romans 12:4-5

We were not created to be alone and live solo.

> We're part of a divine system where everyone is important and plays a different but essential role, individually and as a whole.

Our journey is enriched by others, and through this community and relationships, we are able to uplift each other and thrive.

Whispering SOS

When Nova was born I knew I wanted to breastfeed her, and it was important for me to do so because, before she was born, I did a lot of research on the advantages of breastfeeding. I was convinced it was the best for my baby, but my breastfeeding journey was far from easy.

Nova was born with a condition known as posterior tongue and upper lip tie, which in most cases can disrupt a child's ability to latch properly onto the breast. Most of the time, this condition can negatively impact the breastfeeding experience for mom and baby. In simple words, the mother may experience pain while breastfeeding, and the baby may not be able to latch properly onto the breast and empty it, which in turn results in a low milk supply from the mom, and the baby not gaining enough weight.

We didn't know Nova had this condition during her first few months of life. The pediatrician at the hospital didn't catch it, nor did the nurses or lactation consultants that came to our hospital room to check on her.

Initially, I felt excruciating pain while breastfeeding Nova. I remember when we were still at the hospital, I kept trying to put her on the breast but my nipples got cut open, and the pain was so unbearable that at some point I just couldn't do it anymore, and I stopped.

I was swollen, exhausted, and recovering physically and mentally from a four day long induced labor and an unplanned C-section; but if you are familiar with some of the basics of breastfeeding, you know how important it is to constantly breastfeed your baby those first few days to help your body produce enough milk. In summary, I started my breastfeeding journey on the wrong foot.

The first few days after Nova was born, I didn't stimulate my breast often enough by either latching her on my breast or pumping myself every two hours with an electric breast pump—as they advised me to do—and my breasts gradually stopped producing colostrum, which is the first secretion from the mammary glands after giving birth, rich in antibodies.

I remember the third day while still in the hospital, I tried to breast pump myself and nothing came out. It was as if my breasts got completely dry.

> **I was mortified and felt like I was a failure as a mother—I couldn't produce the one thing my baby needed the most to thrive and I felt guilty about it.**

The whole situation hurt me deeply. I was absolutely heartbroken. After having such a traumatic labor and delivery experience, I craved creating that bond between us both, the mother-daughter bond so many mothers spoke of when they had their first child. I imagined breastfeeding her and watching her fall asleep while being nestled into my chest. It tore my heart in two not being able to experience it. The only thing in life I wanted at that moment was to breastfeed my baby and I couldn't do it.

When I got back home after leaving the hospital, I felt miserable and began to cry. I couldn't stop the sea of tears coming from the bottom of my broken soul. I felt guilty for not focusing on the positive side of things—my baby was perfect and healthy, what else could I ask for?—But I was mourning a birthing experience I envisioned from the beginning of my pregnancy, and now grieving my failed breastfeeding journey. I felt like I was already the worst mother in the world after only having her for a few days.

I didn't know what to do. The whole situation made me feel lonely, hopeless, and defeated.

Eventually, I managed to collect myself enough to reach out to a close friend of mine, Jackie, who had her baby before Nova was born. She was a huge advocate for breastfeeding mothers, and I knew she would be able to offer me some kind of consolation and advice about the whole ordeal.

When I called her, I immediately wished I had reached out to her sooner. She came to see me right away and donated some of her own breast milk for Nova while I recovered. I didn't ask her to do that, and in all honesty, I didn't know a mother would donate their breastmilk to others. I didn't even know donating breast milk was a thing at all, but I was so thankful for it!

When she came to the house after donating her milk, she then put her hands on my shoulders and said something that instantly put my mind at ease:

"I know you're stressed about being completely dry.

Your mental health and inner peace play a huge part in your ability to produce milk for your baby.

You're feeling so much pressure because Nova wasn't being fed with breastmilk as you wanted her to. This is affecting you mentally and emotionally."

Then she continued, "Now that you know she will be having breast milk, you can focus on taking care of yourself. Get some rest, start over tomorrow refreshed and renewed, and the milk will come after. I promise you, it will come." I found comfort and relief in her words, and her support and compassion gave me the strength I needed.

The next morning, I tried the breast pump again and I got my first three drops—yes you read that right, *three single drops*—of colostrum since I was in the hospital. It sounds like so little, but it was a start in the right direction and it meant the world to me. From that day, the amount of breastmilk I was able to produce started to increase by the day, even though I still had to breast pump myself constantly to keep up with it, due to Nova's condition and my low milk supply issues. As much as I was making progress, it was not happening fast enough.

Luckily about a week after, Lilian—a new mom, whom I barely met through a professional environment not too long before that—reached out to me out of nowhere, to check up on me and asked how I was doing. It was almost like God whispered in her heart my SOS.

Inexplicably, I felt like I could open myself to her completely. I explained my breastfeeding situation, the challenges I was facing by having a low milk supply, and the constant breast pumping all day, all night, and every day. How we tried different things with different lactation consultants, and how, even though it was improving, I was still not producing enough milk to exclusively breastfeed Nova. I was tired and discouraged.

Lilian was also so supportive! Again, without me asking for it, she offered to donate breast milk from her bank too. She came to my house a couple of times to deliver them. She was driving around 30 mins each way from her place to mine—with her baby in the car—just to help me and Nova through this hurdle. I now consider Lilian one of my best friends.

God works in mysterious yet powerful ways.

Eventually, when Nova was about two months old, and after several trials and failures, our lactation consultant referred us to a pediatric dentist, who diagnosed the problem right away and fixed it in about ten minutes.

Can you believe it?! I was suffering for two months—eight entire weeks—because we didn't know what the root of the problem was. After the doctor cut these ties, the pain while breastfeeding disappeared, Nova quickly learned how to latch properly, which allowed her to empty my breasts, and I was able to exclusively breastfeed her moving forward. Thankfully, I didn't need any further donations or to continue to breast pump myself anymore.

But looking back, I realize now that if I wouldn't have gone through such difficult experiences, I wouldn't have been vulnerable enough to let others step in and help. I wouldn't have learned the value of leaning on my community, even in such personal and private matters. But most importantly, I wouldn't have been able to help others who are going through similar challenges.

I'm happy to report that my breastfeeding journey turned from being an extremely painful saga to being the most magical fairytale-like adventure I've ever lived.

My prayer is that any mother who wishes to breastfeed her baby can find the amount of support I received from God, friends, family, and professionals around me, so they can overcome any challenges they may encounter, and live in the flesh the extraordinary experience of breastfeeding. Nothing can be compared to it.

In Union There Is Strength

I have always believed there is power within your community and support networks. We can lift each other up when we're down and I was grateful to have people that I could contact when I was feeling overwhelmed with situations. My two mama-friends, Jackie and Lilian, are the perfect examples of it. I don't know what I would have done without them, and I hope they know how much of an impact they both made in my life and Nova's. Yet, my circle of help didn't end with them.

> **One of the biggest mistakes I initially made as a business owner—and as a mother—was to believe I needed to do everything by myself.**

This can't be further from the truth, as there was help and support around me, even in the middle of a pandemic and all the crazy lockdowns, people still came to the rescue whenever we needed it. But at the beginning of my journey, I didn't necessarily understand there was help available to me, and I just needed to ask for it.

Thinking that I was going to have to do it all on my own was part of the reason why I hesitated for so long on starting to have kids. I thought I needed to get all these other personal and professional goals done before starting to grow my family, so I could be able to handle on my own all the responsibilities that come with motherhood.

The truth is, I wish I knew then what I know now. I probably would have started having babies way earlier than I did, because as much as I managed to do on my own, I haven't been alone in this process, and now I see I wouldn't have been alone before or after. I've got support from those around me from day one, and for that I'm thankful.

The old saying rings true here; there is *power in the pack*.

Sometimes I didn't know what to do, sometimes I felt desperate and hopeless, and sometimes I just needed a break. I soon learned when I needed to slow down and seek help. These two things became extremely important in many aspects of my personal and professional life, and they might apply to you too.

You should always try and build up a good support network around you—and use it.

Asking For Help Is a Sign of Wisdom

Feeling comfortable with asking and receiving help from others can be hard for some of us—especially if you're very independent and you're not used to it—but being a mother and a woman in business will most likely take a lot of mental, emotional, and physical energy from you.

It's important to seek and accept help when needed. Nobody should have to do everything on their own. God did not create us to be alone, even less to overcome personal and professional obstacles in complete solitude.

To give you a quick example, architecture is a profession that lives and thrives only through collaboration with others—this is how something mighty is made in the physical world. Have you ever considered how no building has ever been designed and built by one single person? As architects, we need to collaborate with other professionals—structural engineers, mechanical engineers, electrical engineers, plumbing engineers, civil engineers, landscape architects, interior designers, spec writers, manufacturer representatives, general contractors, sub-contractors, vendors, building officials, inspectors, to name a few.

Architecture is an interdisciplinary, collaborative, and creative world. The same can be said for motherhood. We need God, family, friends, healthcare providers, and other professionals to help us so we can survive in our new role and learn how to navigate it better.

If I hadn't called my friend Jackie that night, who knows what might have happened with my breastfeeding journey! I might have ended up feeling worse and worse, blaming myself for not being able to produce milk for Nova, and finally giving up on it. Her kindness and encouragement that night were lifesaving. It had a profound impact on my life and ultimately is what kept me going.

> **Architecture and motherhood are the same in this matter, a healthy community is what makes us stand tall as one.**

This concept can be associated with many other careers, and it definitely applies to any business enterprise.

"But he said to me, "My grace is sufficient for you, for my power is made perfect in weakness." Therefore I will boast all the more gladly about my weaknesses, so that Christ's power may rest on me." 2 Corinthians 12:9

In times of need, wisdom tears our walls down exposing our limitations and vulnerability, so we can be humble enough to ask for help, and within our union with God—and others—we become strong. Allow others to step in. Collaboration with each other is strengthening and reinforcing.

Adaptability Is in Constant Evolution

After having Nova, something that was hard to get used to was that my family—such as my mother, father, and siblings—could not come to visit us as we had originally planned. We had anticipated they would come to our aid after I had Nova to help us adjust to living with a newborn and to give me some extra support in my initial recovery process. Yet, the airports closed and the world went into lockdown because of the COVID-19 pandemic and its restrictions. We felt very lonely at times, but where we couldn't fall back on some people, we had a different support network that was there to help.

Although my side of the family wasn't able to come, my mother-in-law and sisters-in-law didn't live very far from us. As we reached out to them and asked for help here and there, they stepped in to assist us, and honestly, they were extremely helpful. I was sad my family could not fly in to meet Nova and be with us, but Jeremy's side of the family was incredibly giving and supported me just as much.

They went above and beyond, and did things for us I wasn't expecting them to do. They brought us homemade meals and groceries, cleaned the house, did the dishes and the laundry, and even helped me give Nova her first bath, which I was terrified to do on my own. When I felt overwhelmed those first few days, they were there to hold my hand through it all. They were true angels on earth that God sent to my rescue and I was so thankful for everything they did, without ever expecting a single thing in return.

We also had many friends in the area, and they all came and showered Nova with gifts to my surprise! They went out of their way to make sure we didn't feel alone and brought clothes, toys, books, and all kinds of must-have baby things that I didn't know I needed or even existed! Our friends came around and dropped their gifts off at our door with a wave—because of the whole social distancing required during the first few months of the pandemic. Every visit made me feel so looked after by the community around me.

My plans were forcefully changed over and over again. As fiercely independent as I've always been, asking for help was humbling and necessary, but adapting to new scenarios, and moving from a to b, to c on a daily basis with a positive attitude, was just as important. Relying on others rather than my own immediate family brought me opportunities to create unbreakable bonds with others around me that I wouldn't have formed otherwise, and that's the power of adaptability.

> **Your community is there for you in your greatest hour of need.**

Your community is there for you in your greatest hour of need, but even though not every time things will go as anticipated, and maybe those who you truly count on are not able to show up, if you allow yourself to go outside of your comfort zone, other people will rally to your side and bring your way new solutions.

Communicate Through Communication

Even though I had a good support network around me, there was one at home that was irreplaceable. The biggest piece within my support system was my husband, Jeremy, who became a wonderful father and never stopped being an incredible husband. He was my doula during labor, and the amount of work he put in during those four days I was being induced was remarkable.

When I was giving birth to Nova, he held my hand and coached me through the birthing process as I was pushing her out for over four hours. He cried his heart out with me and prayed over me at the edge of the hospital bed when we were told they were going to perform a C-section. He knew how important having a natural birth was for me and how devastating this news was.

Jeremy is also a wonderful father; since we first took Nova home he's been actively involved with her. He would bathe her, change her diaper, rock her to sleep, play with her, clean the house, do laundry, do the dishes, and cook for us. Honestly, the list goes on and on. He is the main and most important piece of my support system and I'm forever thankful that I have him in my life.

However, I now try my best to communicate to him whenever I need help and *how* I need that help to be given by him. This is something that has been an important part of our parenthood journey.

Setting clear expectations is key in any kind of personal or professional relationship you have—but especially in parenthood—so nobody feels frustrated, disappointed, or that their expectations are not being met.

At times, we may feel the person next to us should act in a certain way, or simply assume they should help us with some obvious needs we may have. It might be pretty clear—to us at least—this is how the other person should act or help, without anyone needing to explain anything further to them, right? Wrong. Most of the time people around us want to help but don't know how to do it. If you give them a task and at least some basic guidelines or directions, they will be happy to perform it for you.

Another common mistake is not explaining upfront how you want a task to be done if you're very particular on how you specifically want it. The worst part is when they eventually get around to doing whatever it is you need them to do, but you feel as if they've done it wrong because they didn't do it *your* way. As a result of that, frustration begins to build up for everyone involved—as you feel as though you might as well do it yourself, and the other person may feel unappreciated.

But put yourself in the other person's shoes. It's like expecting a person to climb a tree to fetch an apple, and then getting annoyed that they climbed it using their hands and feet, rather than a ladder—when you never told them you would prefer for them to use a ladder.

The problem with this is we cannot expect someone to do something a certain way without a clear and explicit explanation. Also—and most importantly—keep in mind that sometimes it's better done than perfect. If the end goal is to get the apple, then maybe the means of how they got it down is not necessarily a driving factor, as long as the apple is given to you.

Being open-minded and letting others figure things out in their own way is a leadership quality that many lack.

> **People's minds work in different ways, and we should honor and respect our differences.**

Unfortunately, mind-reading is not available in today's society, so clear and effective communication is the best and safest way to get things done the way you want them. Use this tool abundantly.

Hands-On Training

Nobody has the ability to know how to do everything—it's something we as human beings will never be able to do. There are things to this day that I don't know how to do and probably never will; like riding a unicycle on a tightrope—not that I would particularly want to—but my point here is nobody should be expected to know how to do something out of nowhere, without guidance or proper training.

Being a new parent can feel overwhelming for anyone—although it is incredibly rewarding.

> **We can easily forget our partners are learning—just as we are—how to be the best parents they can be.**

I learned this early on in my motherhood journey.

The day after Nova was born, I couldn't get up from the hospital bed on my own, and Nova's diaper needed to be changed. Jeremy didn't know how to do it—he genuinely didn't, but he tried.

I was watching him do it from the bed and I silently cringed from all the mistakes he was making, so I started directing him from afar. I was frustrated he wasn't doing it right, and I unconsciously started being bossy with him. This was not helpful at all. My bad attitude and judgment made him feel more nervous, and he ended up making a mess, getting Nova's poop everywhere on the changing station.

Due to his first time changing her diaper being such a disaster, the next time Nova needed to get her diaper changed, my first impulse was to get up and do it myself. I didn't want to deal with the mess afterward, and I thought: *if you want it done right, you just have to do it yourself.* Let me tell you right here, this is the wrong mentality to have for anything in life. I think God felt it was about time to give me a small lesson.

Right at that moment, a nurse came into our room. She needed to take Nova's weight to make sure she was healthy and on track, and she needed us to get Nova naked, including taking her diaper off. Jeremy stood there still feeling anxious while trying to figure out what to do.

The nurse noticed Jeremy was struggling, and how I was about to jump to the rescue—when quite honestly, I couldn't even move on my own yet due to my C-Section—so she intervened instead. Patiently and with a great deal of compassion, she showed him how to change Nova's dirty diaper, while ensuring she gave him the proper information and tools he needed to succeed in such a task without making any unnecessary messes.

As silly as it may sound, that experience was a major turning point, and a life lesson for me as a woman, mother, wife, architect, leader, and business owner. Today Jeremy changes Nova's diapers faster and better than I do—which is a lot to say because I'm pretty good at it.

> **I have learned and tried my best to not only communicate far better but to give hands-on training whenever needed.**

I learned this especially after what happened that day in the hospital and how different the nurse's approach was from mine. She was a great coach to Jeremy, but even more to me. I learned from her how unfair I was to Jeremy, and how my answer to every difficulty didn't need to be doing everything myself to *get it done right*, but that I needed to take the time to guide others positively and effectively, and ultimately, help them so they could help me.

Choose What Works Best for You

Another important part of my support system is my mother-in-law, Sandy. I would first like to say that I am extremely blessed to have her in my life. In fact, I've heard many stories of women having issues with their mother-in-laws but this has never been my case, on the contrary, my relationship with Sandy is almost as if she was my own mother and best friend at the same time. Jeremy's parents are the reason why he is the wonderful, compassionate man he is, and it's so easy to see it by just spending time with them.

They are the kindest and sweetest human beings I've ever had the pleasure of meeting and I'm honored to call them my family now. Not only are they giving and compassionate, but they have supported me, as well as Jeremy in so many ways, to the point that I now call them Mom and Dad.

Due to the pandemic, we were not able to get Nova into daycare. They were all closed and not taking new clients, so at the time it was not an option for us. Initially, I was able to handle things on my own, however, when my business and projects were beginning to pick up, there were times when I really needed to have a couple of hours to solely focus on my business. With daycare being out of the equation, we needed to review what other options we had.

Initially, we looked for a nanny to take care of Nova for a couple of hours, two or three days per week. Unfortunately, it was completely unsustainable, as it was quite expensive and we needed something long-term that we could afford consistently.

At the time, Sandy, my mother-in-law, had a pet-sitting business that slowed down drastically due to the pandemic. We were in need of help, but also trying to help her as well, so we asked her if she wished to spend more time with her granddaughter and make some extra money while doing it. Luckily she said yes, so it was a win-win situation for everyone!

Nova got to spend time with one of her grandparents, and it had the added benefit of helping out my mother-in-law during a difficult time.

There was also the fact that having her around Nova was a blessing and it gave me peace of mind. Sandy raised the sweetest man I know, Jeremy. She had also managed to raise four other boys, all of which are smart, successful, and just as kind as Jeremy is. I knew that in her hands, Nova was going to be safe and loved.

Now, with her support, I was able to get some time to focus on my business each week, without compromising the quality of my time with Nova.

> **Your support system can make or break you. It's an essential piece of the puzzle to find the balance between motherhood and business.**

My options may differ from yours, and what works for me may not work for you, and that is ok. Do what works best for you and your family. It's *your* journey, not anyone else's. Take the time to figure out who is part of your support system and how you can incorporate them into your schedule and routines.

You may find support from your spouse, your family, friends, co-workers, postpartum doulas, support groups, healthcare providers, public or private institutions, and so on. Find them, understand your options, and for God's sake, use them!

You don't have to walk on this journey alone. Let others help.

YOUR TURN:

1. When was a time you felt empowered through others?

   _____

   _____

2. How have you been able to adapt whenever your plans have changed?

   _____

   _____

3. How can you improve the way you communicate your needs to others?

   _____

   _____

4. What support system works best for you?

   _____

   _____

TAKEAWAYS:

- Motherhood is not about doing everything on your own, nor is business.
- Asking for help signals you're strong enough to recognize you need it.
- Adaptability and improvisation are a form of art.
- The best way to get the results you're expecting is by clearly communicating your expectations.
- What works for you is what works for you. Own it!

Draw Your Thoughts

Grow Your Support System

"A thriving environment is where your weaknesses are balanced out by others' *strengths.*"

Gloria Kloter

Chapter 7

Lead through Self-Awareness

One can only know and do so much, but many people presume that if you're not good at something you won't be good at anything, and you should keep trying until things eventually slide into place. It would be great if everyone was good at everything, but that's not the reality of things.

> **We have different talents in different areas for a reason. I consider this part of God's perfect plan for us, so we need one another.**

The mystery to solve is within, to set ourselves up for success, so we all can *glow* individually and as a whole in business and in life.

Sleeping Beauty

I always joke with my husband about how I don't understand why newborns fight their sleep so much. Sleeping is the best thing in the world, right?!

There's nothing better than climbing into bed under a soft comforter after a long day of work, then closing your eyes and drifting off to sleep. Of course, I am probably romanticizing sleep a little bit. Admittedly—more so after I became a new mother. Sleep deprivation is something the majority of new parents experience, and after going through it all, I have a higher level of appreciation for a good night's sleep.

> Sleep deprivation is something the majority of new parents experience.

When I was studying architecture—and during the first few years of my career—I used to pull lots of all-nighters for work, and I always was able to handle myself perfectly fine the next day. But things have changed drastically, I don't have the ability to do such things anymore. I consider sleeping to be almost sacred nowadays. As a new parent sleeping becomes a luxury, and it's something I try not to take for granted anymore, which I used to do many years ago.

Yet, I cannot complain. Jeremy and I are extremely blessed in that sense. Nova has been one of those rare babies who sleeps long hours since her early days, but quite honestly, not everything has been just a matter of good luck, as we took the "Taking Cara Babies" online class.[1]

We learned a few tricks on how to get her to sleep through the night since she was two weeks old. The things they teach in the class really worked for Nova. However, even though she sleeps this long, at first she used to struggle big time with falling asleep by herself whenever we put her down for the night.

At times, I'd get the sense that maybe she thought something was wrong when she was getting tired. It was almost as if she was fearful of sleeping in a way. Have you experienced anything like it with a baby before?

She would fight and cry until she couldn't anymore, and by the time she was finally down, I would feel drained and exhausted by the process of helping her settle. Worn down by her fighting the world and the audacity of me trying to gently rock her to sleep without collapsing myself.

There are things we are just not good at doing. Yet, on the other hand, there are things that even if we're perfectly capable of doing, know how to do them, and we may even be good at doing, we just loathe doing them—and that is completely *okay*. No guilt or shame should be felt for it.

> **We all have weaknesses and strengths that make us who we are. The key is understanding where ours lie, so we can play to our strengths more than to our weaknesses.**

I usually feel drained when I'm doing something I don't enjoy. It feels like I'm constantly dragging myself to do it. It's ok if I have to do it from time to time, but it's not sustainable long-term.

This is why your thriving capabilities are intimately laced with your self-awareness.

Don't get me wrong, many things are worth fighting for, and you should never throw in the towel before giving yourself the chance to try first, especially if it's something important for you to do and you are passionate about. My architecture licensing process in the US and my breastfeeding journey are two great examples of it. Failing repeatedly initially in something doesn't mean you won't be able to master it. If there's something your heart desires, please go for it and try it as long as necessary, because those are not the type of tasks and challenges I'm talking about here.

> **My point is if you don't enjoy doing something, either if you're good at it or not, why should you keep spending time and energy on it?**

One of my biggest weaknesses overall is my lack of patience, especially if I'm physically or mentally tired, and during the first few months of having Nova, I was definitely both. My sleep deprivation played a big role in my struggle with getting her to sleep. I wished for her to fall asleep sooner and easier, so I could get some sleep myself.

Why couldn't I get her to fall asleep faster and peacefully? What was I doing wrong? What was I missing?

Slowly, I became aware I wasn't patient enough in this matter. I absolutely loved rocking my baby and snuggling with her, but by the end of the day I was already so tired I didn't have anything else to give, and her fighting sleep was something out of my control.

The only thing to be done was to help her by being loving and patient, and I was lacking the latter of these two.

I watched Jeremy rock her to sleep a couple of times, he was so calm and peaceful at it. Maybe he wasn't as tired as I was, or maybe that's a strength he had that I didn't.

I talked to him to find a solution that would work for the two of us. I expressed my feelings and concerns, and how I needed help. We agreed on modifying her nightly routine to give her a bath together, he would put on her diaper and pajamas, I would breastfeed her after, and then he would rock her to sleep.

That way there was a balance, we both spent time with her at night, and it meant I was no longer feeling physically and mentally drained. It's pointless to try and wage a war against your weaknesses—in the end, the best thing to do is to talk openly about what you're struggling with and find a solution for it.

Sleep is a part of life, and as much as Nova wanted to stay awake—eventually, as she became more active while learning to sit, crawl, stand, and finally walk—she slowly improved and got to the point where she went to sleep pretty easily and on her own. And just like that, she enjoyed going to bed just as much as we did.

The Strength of Knowing Your Weakness

Overall, having self-awareness is important in both your personal and professional life, to recognize where you should and shouldn't be focusing your time and energy.

In terms of my business, my strengths lay deeper in the design side of things… You know, the creative stuff! My happy place is when I'm working on the schematic design phase of my projects and doing the initial space planning.

I have lots of fun playing around with the exterior elevations, but the one thing I love the most is working on the interiors. I also have great skills in dealing with building codes, project management, client relations, permitting processes, and construction administration, among other things.

Yet, as much as I embraced my strengths—I needed to ensure I was also aware of my weaknesses and didn't put a strain on myself by taking on more than I could handle.

Saying I am horrible at anything admin-related is probably an understatement. I don't like having to deal with the paperwork, spreadsheets, invoicing, contracts, insurances, taxes, and the list goes on and on. Every time I have to do these tasks, I feel bored and exhausted from even thinking about it! I would make excuses to avoid them and even procrastinate. I'm capable of doing it, but I'm not my best at it because I hate doing it. There, I said it! I HATE doing it!

These kinds of tasks feel as if they are not in my nature—I thrive at many different things but administrative paperwork just isn't one of them. Quite honestly, I think a lot of architects may feel the same way about this; we are creative by nature, and as such heavy paperwork just drains away from our abilities.

There are so many administrative tasks that come with managing a business, and even if it's a part of your everyday life, it doesn't make it any easier if it's not your thing.

Of course, admin tasks must be done, they are essential for any business. The same can be said of any other tasks you may feel are not enjoyable in general, someone has to do them. I think it is ok if you have to do it yourself initially—or if you have to step in whenever it's needed later on—but it shouldn't be the norm.

So, how could I stay focused on the things I was good at and enjoyed the most and avoid falling into the trap of constantly forcing myself to do the things that made me feel miserable when doing them?

I talked to my husband for his insight, as he has a background in business. We analyzed the list of tasks that I needed help with, the amount of time needed to get them done, and a fair price to pay for those hours of work.

After some quick calculations, Jeremy proved to me how delegating these tasks and paying for someone else to do them made much more sense than me trying it on my own. I was able to outsource the hardest parts of my day to someone with the right set of skills, who was able to complete these tasks way faster and more efficiently than me.

> **In retrospect, if I didn't understand my weaknesses, I would have tried to force myself to excel at the things that I am just not that good at.**

I would have been constantly feeling like a failure because my expectations were unrealistic, and my time would have been spent in the wrong place. Instead, I now focus my energy on the things I truly enjoy doing, and where I can thrive the most.

If I continued trying to perform those tasks I struggled with, I would have felt burnt out sooner than later—and that's what happens when you constantly force yourself to do what you don't want to do, it always feels like a bad job, even if you're working on your own business.

Like any other human, I could list my strengths to no end. Though admitting your weaknesses can be a lot harder, it's just as important. Embracing your weaknesses is one of the first steps toward success.

The School of Life

Looking back, I have always felt like they don't teach us enough about business administration, the business of architecture, architectural practice, or even marketing strategies in architecture school. At least, this was the case for me where I studied. I know of many other women in other types of business avenues who are dealing with similar issues within their career paths.

> **In college you learn so much about your career but not so much about how to run a business of it.**

In my case, while I was in architecture school I learned mostly about design. My creativity was challenged to its bare core, and the courses managed to cover many different aspects of it, but it never seemed to be enough information to prepare me to be a business owner. After I graduated, I felt like I lacked knowledge in so many different business management-related things, which I needed to master in order to run a successful business.

This is why I believe a lot of small-business owners end up going back into the corporate world after trying to *make it* on their own. A lot of us hit a wall when starting a business due to the lack of proper training on how to manage one. The worst part is, most of the time, you don't learn these skills in your typical job either, because it's not in their best interest if you go out on your own.

This is unfair to us in general, it means that from the beginning we do not have the tools we need to succeed independently and we're forced to either work for others forever or learn to run our business the hard way. The latest was the case for me in both the Dominican Republic and Florida.

Granted, there are lots of architects and women in other types of careers who prefer to stay within the corporate world—but for those of us who envision working for ourselves, it feels like you're trying to draw blood from a stone trying to navigate it all. It shouldn't be this way.

If you feel this way, just know that you're not the exception to the rule. This is a very common struggle that many of us face, and the best learning experiences you'll have are the ones you'll get through the school of life.

Delegating and Outsourcing

Have you ever heard the real estate phrase, "There are three things that matter in property: Location, location, location," by Harold Samuel?

> **When thinking of tools to ease your professional life and motherhood, the first thing that comes to my mind is** *delegate, delegate, delegate.*

In motherhood and business, relying on your "team of experts" is critical to success and finding these individuals is a form of art on its own. A good example of this in the built environment is the necessary cooperation between architects and their design team.

This team is not limited to employees within their companies, but it usually branches out to include other individuals who complement the architect's skills and expertise. Examples of these are interior designers, engineers, manufacturers representatives, general contractors, and other professionals that assist us in the design process. Ultimately they distribute the load when dealing with bidding, permitting, or the construction administration phases as well.

Delegating while running a business is also fundamental. While I am aware that not everyone is able to hire others right when they're starting their business, it's important that you make it part of your plan, even if the vision you have for your business is to stay within a small number of team members. Don't get trapped in trying to do everything on your own forever. It's not worth it.

> **A thriving environment is where your weaknesses are balanced out by others' strengths. This can be said in business and motherhood as well.**

There are many ways to make it work in today's world. You can hire a virtual assistant to help with administrative tasks, get a Certified Public Accountant (CPA) to help with bookkeeping and tax-related duties, you could pay per hour to a consultant to help you with specific tasks for a couple of hours per week, or you could even hire a full-time employee to delegate some of your workloads.

I chose to do some of the above, in various different areas of my business. An example of this is production, which in itself could be tedious work. However, it is a large part of an architect's job and could be extremely time-consuming.

As my business started to grow, production was stealing time away from other things I also needed to do, such as focusing on design, solving life-safety related challenges in the projects, making sure everything was up to code, selecting materials and systems, bringing in new clients and finding new projects to take on.

I understood very quickly that doing all the production by myself was actually holding me back. I needed to delegate it at least partially.

Initially, I wasn't ready to hire full-time employees yet, so I decided to start by finding two talented individuals to help me with production and graphics remotely. I needed to ensure I hired people who had the same high standards and could produce the same quality of work that I did. After doing some research, I found the perfect team members who met my expectations.

By having them on board, I was able to better focus on client generation, marketing strategies, business development, the design process, and overseeing what my team was doing in different stages of the projects. It allowed me to give them the support and direction they needed while taking care of our clients and projects more efficiently.

> **Delegating things made it far easier for me to manage my business and allowed things to run far smoother.**

Oftentimes, I hear the saying—*practice makes perfect*—and this rings true in a lot of cases. However, if you're continuously practicing something, but after trying your best you still find it wearing and taxing, then it might be time to outsource those tasks to someone else. Practice may lead to perfect—but delegation makes life far more efficient.

YOUR TURN:

1. What are the things you enjoy doing the most as a mother and as a business woman?
   _____
   _____

2. What things drain you the most in your personal life and at work?
   _____
   _____

3. Can you delegate any of the above to anyone in your support circle?
   _____
   _____

4. How can you start outsourcing the things you are not able to handle on your own effectively anymore?
   _____
   _____

TAKEAWAYS:

- You're special for the things you know as well as for what you don't. It makes you who *you* are.
- Being aware of your strengths and weaknesses will help you set realistic expectations for yourself.
- There's no better teacher than your own experiences.
- There's beauty within splitting the weight with others.

Draw Your Thoughts

"*Stress* will manage you unless you manage it."

Gloria Kloter

Chapter 8

Organize the Chaos

Being a successful mother and woman in business doesn't necessarily mean you're successful at looking after yourself.

> There's still an individual inside of you who has needs, dreams, and aspirations that may not be necessarily related to work or motherhood.

When we forget our existence and importance is when turmoil starts piling up until chaos explodes in our faces. My chaos cut deep through my essence and I didn't see it coming.

Hesitancy and Doubts

By the time Nova was turning one year old, Jeremy and I were back and forth talking about if we wanted to try for a second baby.

This is a decision that a lot of couples struggle with. For some, the decision is very easy and straightforward, they know for a fact they want a bigger family, but that wasn't necessarily the case for us.

> **Making the decision of having a second baby was very personal to me in many ways.**

First, as I explained in previous chapters, I had a very traumatic labor experience while being induced. I spent a couple of days in labor in a hospital that limited all my options due to COVID restrictions at the time.

There was a part of me that wanted a second chance to heal emotionally from it. Deep inside me, I longed for a smoother experience that I could look back to, without feeling pain or a sense of grief and mourning. There was also another part of me still in the process of healing physically, recovering from diastasis recti, and other issues that came with having an unplanned C-Section.

Even though having a second baby was a decision that needed to be done by the two of us, I felt that in the end, it was on me to decide if I was ready or not for it. It was my body, my mental health, and my emotions that would be jeopardized again.

If you also feel this way, know that you're not alone. Not everyone is ready to have more babies right away, or at all. The fact that our bodies are God's vessels to create life is magical, but this wonderful process also takes a toll on us.

You may think I'm crazy, but there was also this other part of me that felt a sense of guilt when thinking of having a second child. It's hard to put it into words, but the best way I can describe it is that I felt like I was betraying Nova for wanting a second baby.

The thought of splitting my love and attention made me feel guilty. I was concerned about her feeling less loved or jealous.

I was torn.

On the other hand, I watched Nova's behavior around other children. Her sweet and playful soul would be pulled towards them so naturally and effortlessly. She's naturally a social butterfly. It melts my heart to see her around other kids. She would hug them, kiss them, share her food and toys, dance, and play with them with the warmest love and care.

There was this part of me that could visualize her with siblings, and how happy she would be with a best friend and companion. That part of me wanted a second baby and it grew stronger than any of my fears.

Out of My Control

By the time we felt we were somewhat ready to start trying to conceive again, we thought it was going to be as easy as it was the first time. The first time we tried to conceive was during our trip to Europe and two weeks later we magically got a big fat positive pregnancy test.

I must confess, unconsciously I took that miraculous experience for granted as I mistakenly thought conceiving babies was always going to be easy for us. Little did I know how wrong I was.

Things looked very different the second time around. One month came, then the next one, and then the one after, and we didn't get pregnant.

It was only a couple of months, but it gave me a sense of failure. It made me feel broken.

> **There's nothing more powerful than realizing you can't have something at the time you wish to have it, to make you want it even more and above all other things.**

For the first time in my life, I started paying real attention to how ovulation works, the complexity of it, and all the parts and pieces needed to fall into place for a pregnancy to happen. The more I learned about my body, the more empowered I felt and the more in awe I continued to be about the marvelous beings women are. It still blows my mind to witness how God created us in such a detailed and perfect way, and what a miracle it is to conceive a baby.

Finally, after seven months of trying, I got a positive pregnancy test early in December! I was so excited that our family was going to expand and how much joy this new baby was going to bring into our lives. This baby was so wanted and instantly loved. We made so many fun plans on how we were going to tell the family the good news on Christmas night while opening gifts, and we daydreamed about their funny reactions.

Our joy didn't last long. When I was about six weeks pregnant I started spotting. Spotting rapidly progressed into a full flow that night. I lost our precious baby and there was nothing I could do about it.

I remember I had to attend a work-related event that same evening.

> **Being around people, smiling and keeping it together while knowing I was having a miscarriage after we were trying to conceive for so long, taught me about the level of resiliency we women can endure.**

I found support and consolation after speaking with family and friends about it. Many of them expressed going through similar situations in the past—which I had no idea about—and hearing their experiences made me feel less lonely.

Two months later, just when I was finally starting to overcome my deep state of grief, I got pregnant for a second time… Only to miscarriage not too long after again. My heart was completely shattered and my faith was shaken.

These devastating experiences took me into a dark place, a side of me I didn't know I had. I couldn't get out of the sense of loss, guilt, depression, anger, disappointment, and heartbrokenness.

I kept questioning myself, rewinding everything I did during the weeks before it happened, and wondering over and over *what if?* What if I wouldn't have done this or that? What if I wouldn't have eaten this or drank that? What if it was all my fault? What if I'm not able to have more children?

The truth is, I don't know the answer to any of those questions and maybe I never will, it's all out of my control. The one thing I know for sure is God is in control. I was neglecting myself while trying to figure things out on my own, but God only knows why, if, when, and how in my story. I needed to stand still and trust him by letting go and focusing on my relationship with Him to find healing, hope, encouragement, and comfort in His presence.

I let go, and let God.

One thing that really helped us get through this was reading the book "Loved Baby" by Sarah Philpott. This is a compilation of 31 devotionals and other stories from women who had experienced miscarriages to help us grieve and cherish our children after pregnancy loss.

Stress Management

During my recovery journey, I discovered a lot of things about myself, one of which was how my progesterone levels were low due to my stress levels being extremely high. Unlike getting pregnant or avoiding a miscarriage, one thing within my power was the ability to manage my levels of stress so I decided to do something about it.

Initially, when I opened my business, I took on a couple of new clients and projects that ultimately differed from what ended up being our ideal ones, and it added a lot of unnecessary stress to my business and life in general and it completely disrupted my daily routine. Those first few months there was so much chaos and unconsciously I put myself last in line.

I was surrounded by stress of my own making and was in a place where everything exhausted me, but instead of taking a break, I kept digging deeper and deeper. I let my business overpower my personal life.

I see now that even though I was successful in many ways, I wasn't as successful in looking after myself, and it wasn't until the miscarriages happened that I realized how severely this was affecting my health. It was a wake-up call, and I knew something needed to change moving forward.

> **Stress will manage you unless you manage it.**

My miscarriages forced me to slow down and rethink how I was handling my life. Have you ever heard the old saying "you can't pour from an empty cup?" I needed to organize my chaos in order to take care of myself first, so I could take care of others.

Please don't get me wrong, by organizing my chaos I don't necessarily mean my house was always spotlessly clean—believe me, it was quite the opposite many times since Nova was born—but if there's one thing I can tell for a fact that motherhood helped me improve exponentially in my professional life, it was how to be more structured and organized.

Yet I wasn't being intentional enough to apply these principles to myself as an individual. I was paying attention to the mother and business owner, but not so much to Gloria, the woman who had an independent identity between those two.

I remember there were days early on in my motherhood journey when I would wake up with Nova's cry. I would jump from my bed, run to her bedroom, pick her up, feed her, change her diaper, put on her clothes, play with her, and finally put her to sleep again for another 60 minutes.

By that time, it was already mid-morning or even noon and I was still without brushing my teeth, having a shower, breakfast, or even a glass of water, and don't even mention exercising. Working out was a distant thought in my mind at that time. Initially, I was all over the place, focused on figuring things out and dealing with the breastfeeding obstacles.

By the time I started the business, things had improved. Breastfeeding was solved, I had help with Nova and a good rhythm with my initial workload. I was organized and on track, but then I filled up my schedule with more and more work and that's when things started to go downhill.

When I had the miscarriages, I remember feeling like I was always wired.

> **I didn't know how to mentally unplug from my business responsibilities.**

I had issues falling asleep. I would dream about my projects and the challenges that arose in some of them, and I would wake up feeling tired and restless all day long. Looking back I was so overworked, it's so obvious now, but I didn't see it while I was in the middle of it all.

ME Time

Through this experience, I learned I needed to find ways to disconnect and refocus on myself in order to refuel my energy and sense of well-being. The best way I accomplished this was by scheduling and prioritizing the time I would spend on myself. As simple as it sounds, it actually took a lot of effort to figure things out, actually do it, and most importantly, continuing to do it.

For an everyday routine, I started by deciding on how I would like my day to go and I tried to stick to it as much as I could. Running a business and being a new mother meant that I might not always be able to do it all as planned, but a schedule would mean that my life would run far smoother than it would without it.

After a few days, I had a schedule in place for mornings and nights, and it changed my entire perspective on how to live my life. There was something thrilling about having a tiny portion of the day for me alone, where I was giving myself time to fully wake up, spend quiet time with God, reflect on the things I was thankful for, workout, get a nice hot shower, pamper myself, and plan the rest of the things I needed to accomplish that particular day.

I would end the day by focusing on truly relaxing my mind and body, so I could disconnect from everything else and rest.

My morning and night schedule ended up being very similar throughout the week.

I started practicing what I called *me time*.

It was helpful and effective, and overall it looked pretty much like this:

- The number one and most important change I made was starting to wake up before everyone else in my house, to give myself a few hours alone. This was a driving factor for everything else to go as planned, and it made all the difference. Before, whenever I woke up it would be at the same time as Nova.

   From this, I wouldn't have any time for myself and I would feel behind for the rest of the day. I just couldn't catch up.

The best way I was able to accomplish this change on a regular basis was by being extremely disciplined on going to bed consistently around the same time. Many times in the past I made the mistake of staying up too late working on something that—in my head—couldn't wait until the next day, and this always screwed up my entire schedule. By making my bedtime early enough and consistent each night, I was able to fully rest and wake up renewed. It made all the difference!

- Once I was awake, I would spend time reading the Bible, reflecting on my daily devotionals, and praying. I would close my eyes and thank God for all the blessings in my life—my baby, husband, puppies, family, friends, health, home, business, and all the opportunities and growth. I would present my struggles, fears, and wishes before Him and ask for wisdom and direction for the day, and for Him to use me to be a blessing to others.

- Next, I would exercise. Most days I would start by taking a walk outdoors to warm up and let myself get in contact with nature. After that, I would work out at home by following videos inside an app I had on my phone which was exclusively tailored for postpartum moms, and I would finish by stretching.

- After exercising I would take a nice long hot shower. I don't know if you feel the same way, but being able to have a nice long shower has always been a way for me to just start my day right!

- After my shower, I would take some time to do my hair and makeup for the day. It could be something very simple, but to me, it always felt like a pampering session; feeling all dolled up for the day provided me with high self-esteem.

Nothing makes me feel more empowered than feeling beautiful in my own way. It would also make me feel refreshed, energized, and ready to take on the world.

- The next thing I would do is to prepare a cup of tea and spend a couple of minutes reviewing my calendar and schedule, and carefully updating my to-do list for the day. Taking the time for it was crucial for me. Here are a couple of reasons why:

A to-do list is one of the most important tools I use to organize and plan my day.

1. Having a to-do list in place makes it almost impossible to miss anything. It also helps you prioritize important tasks and you are held accountable over the course of the day. It can make all the long, arduous tasks that come with building a business and a life for yourself more manageable. A lot of the time, I would break down large tasks into bite-sized chunks, which in turn makes them look more enticing to complete.

2. Not to mention, it also feels far better when you check off each part of the long task list. One of the biggest advantages I personally have found on the actual motion of ticking things off a list is that it gives you a sense of accomplishment, and it will motivate you to take on the next task.

3. Last but not least, a to-do list gives you credit and acknowledgment. Even if you don't get to finish every single item on the list, it helps you visualize everything you actually have accomplished, so you don't feel like

a failure by the end of the day. Progress is progress, no matter how fast or slow we go.

- Next, I would prepare breakfast for me and my family when everyone else was just beginning to wake up.

- The last step was always getting inside Nova's room. Seeing her smile first thing in the morning is priceless. I would change her diaper, put on clothes for the day, do her hair and feed her.

And that way I always felt I was ahead of the day, instead of behind.

After having a full day of work—sometimes from home, sometimes from the office—I would stop working around 4:00 pm and spend the rest of the time exclusively with Nova until she was down for the night. No phones or computers around, all of my attention was hers.

Spending time with Nova was always a priority and it gave me so much joy that it felt therapeutic.

Babies have this way of bringing you happiness by just being themselves.

After Nova was down for the night, I also followed a night routine to help myself wine down and relax even further. This nightly schedule usually looked like this:

- I would spend quality time with Jeremy, and engage in conversations about our day, challenges, victories, future plans, and such.

- Then I would dim all the lights at home.

- Play some relaxing/ Zen type of music in the background.
- Do some stretching exercises, practice mindfulness, deep breathing, or yoga.
- Take a hot shower and use aromatherapy soaps.
- Make a cup of caffeine-free teas. My favorite was natural ginger root with cinnamon tea.
- Read a book that is not related to my work. Inspirational and self-development books are usually my favorite, but I also like to read about anything that enriches my knowledge and uplifts my soul in general.
- Read the Bible and reflect on my nightly devotion.
- And finally go to sleep, as much as possible at the same time every night.

My way might not be your way, and that's ok.

> **Just be aware of the need to allocate time for yourself and your family, however that looks like for you.**

Spending quality time with my daughter and husband, and having a bit of time to myself each day was the best change I made. The time that was purely for me meant that I was putting myself first for a brief period of time—and this was something I needed to prioritize moving forward.

Some General Rules

Making time for myself was half of the battle, but there were so many other things within my days that I also needed to monitor and improve on. You may or may not identify with some of the following, but this is a list of simple rules I set for myself which helped me to stay on track, be more productive while working, and ultimately allocate time for other things that were also important for me:

- Schedule the time you'll check your emails. In the past, I've made the mistake of checking and responding to my emails right away. It's distracting and time-consuming. What works best for me is to allocate specific times during the day to take care of them. I usually check my emails early in the morning, right after lunch, and before I stop working by the end of the day. I try to spend about 30-minutes each time and address anything that's time-sensitive first. If there's anything I'm not able to address at the time, I either mark the email as unread as a reminder to go over it later, or I send an email to the person letting them know I'm working on it and I'll get back to them within a reasonable time.

- Put your phone away. Yes, when we're talking about spending too much time on your phone, scrolling down social media, or chatting with family and friends, I'm guilty as charged. For that reason when I'm working I put my phone away. Don't get me wrong, I take phone calls as soon as they come in, as most of the time they're from clients and they're important, but I don't chat or use my social media at any other time besides my breaks. This is completely separate from the time I invest in social media for my business marketing.

Procrastination is a sign of our fear of failure.

- Avoid procrastination. I recently attended one of the Young Architect Conferences and learned that procrastination is a sign of our fear of failure. We tend to procrastinate if we feel afraid or intimidated by the task we need to perform. We can also procrastinate if the task itself is something we don't enjoy doing, among other reasons. This knowledge made me be more aware, and now whenever I find myself procrastinating I consciously take the time to analyze why I am avoiding the task.

  If my issue is with something I don't want to do long-term, then I start planning for ways to delegate it. If the root of my problem is fear—of not being smart enough, or doing something wrong and feeling humiliated after… You know, all of those impostor syndrome types of thoughts we all have from time to time—then one thing that has worked best for me is to reach out to my mentors, discuss with them my thoughts and doubts, and ask for advice and guidance on the matter. Don't forget that it takes a village in both, motherhood and business. There's no point in trying to figure everything out on your own.

- No computer or phone after a specific hour. I know sometimes this one is hard to stick to, but we should avoid working at night; it's just not good for us in general. Being in front of your computer and phone during late hours can drastically impact your body's ability to produce melatonin, a natural hormone your body uses to sleep.

  I understand that sometimes we have deadlines to meet and the work must be done, but it should be the exception, not the norm. For those out-of-the-norm occasions when you absolutely have to work at night, my advice is to set up your computer and phone screens to activate the night shift which changes the screen lighting and brightness to be warmer. Your phone may already have an embedded option for it. I currently use an iPhone and it's in the display and brightness settings. For my computer, I installed a software called F.LUX which modifies my screen to be warmer in the timeframe I schedule it for.

> **If you have to work during the weekends on a consistent basis then something needs to be revised.**

- No work on weekends. This one has laced up together with the rule above, and it's particularly hard to follow for those who are business owners. Hear me out on this, if you have to work during the weekends on a consistent basis then something needs to be revised. You might be taking more work than you can handle, need an extra team member, or are pricing your work below its real worth for you to be able to distribute the load with others.

  If none of these apply, then something could be stealing the time away from you when you're supposed to be getting that work done instead. One of these thieves could be some level of procrastination. Do your own checks and balances and take care of this issue as soon as possible.

- Simplify the household chores where you can. Sometimes that means putting all the dishes in the dishwasher instead of washing them manually, meal prepping once or twice a week versus cooking every day, delegating some of those duties to someone within your support system—like your spouse... *HINT, HINT!*—or even trying to temporarily pay someone to clean or meal prep for you. If you can afford it, there are companies who exclusively dedicate themselves to that type of service, and even if you can't use them on a consistent basis just know they're an option.

My favorite tip in this matter I learned from my dear friend, mentor, and role model, Joanna La Bounty, from my Young Architect family. She explained how she splits the household chores and distributes them throughout the week, so they become quicker and easier to perform each day instead of being a long and heavy commitment at a time. What a brilliant idea! Anything you can do to cut time with these tasks will lift some of the burdens off you.

- Learn to say NO without guilt. I'm a natural overachiever and I tend to say yes to too many things.

> **Motherhood and business ownership have taught me to say no to anything that's outside of my own boundaries, disrupts my baby's schedule drastically, or doesn't benefit others.**

I've also learned to say no to clients and projects that won't align with our vision and business. We've learned the hard way that sometimes we win by losing and letting go. Not every client and project is good for you, so focus your energy and time on those who actually are.

With that being said, I utterly believe we rise by lifting others. I do sacrifice certain things and say yes if I feel that by doing so I will be of service to my community or to the profession of architecture and the built environment as a whole. We may be inclined to think we'll feel fulfilled by always getting, taking, and receiving, but God has taught me that true fulfillment can only be found in giving.

- Be reasonable. Filling up my day with more than I can handle means that I'm setting myself up for failure. When I'm working on my to-do list in the mornings, I've become more critical of what's realistic to accomplish. Understanding that things pop up unexpectedly throughout the day has taught me to leave room for error, and I now see the red flags ahead when I'm adding way too many things to my day. Also, setting up realistic expectations includes understanding how the time I spend with Nova in the mornings, afternoon, and evenings are not only sacred, but they're enough.

> **Knowing that I don't need to be with her 24/7 to feel I'm being a good mother is as essential as not feeling guilty for spending time with myself.**

- Keep learning and growing. Allocate time for your personal and professional growth. Read books with something new you can learn, attend local lectures or presentations related to your career, or register for the next conference in your field. Make sure you're always up to date with your industry and stay current with whatever the new trends are.

- Drink more water. This one might sound like an obvious one and too basic to even be a part of this list, but in all honesty, I struggle a lot with drinking enough water throughout the day—I can go a full day with merely a glass or two of water, and it is a constant battle for me. Recently I found out how many people also struggle with this issue, and as you may know, nothing good comes from being dehydrated.

  A tip I learned years ago while I was taking a memorization class was to drink one or two glasses of water right after waking up, to help your body and brain hydrate from being the entire night before with minimum to no liquids. I also use a water bottle called "Hidrate" which pairs with an app on my phone. This water bottle glows and also sends notifications to my phone to remind me to drink water every so often, and it tracks the amount of water I've drank throughout the day. Drink away my friend, your body will thank you later.

- Vacations, recreation, hobbies, and your bucket list.

> **Life doesn't stop because you have a job or own a business and suddenly become a mom.**

You are still allowed to plan for your vacations and tick things off your bucket list—with and without your children. Jeremy and I try to take several vacations a year, some with Nova visiting family and friends, and some just the two of us—even if it's just a quick weekend in Miami which is a couple of hours from where we live. I also started scheduling my appointments ahead of time to get my hair, lashes, manicure, and pedicure done.

- Plan for time with your spouse. As I mentioned above, I spend quality time with Jeremy as much as possible. One thing that's constant on a regular basis is our Friday date night. We may get a babysitter to stay home while Nova is asleep, or we may just order food and watch a movie together, either way, it's a time we spend together as a couple to close out the week right.

- Celebrate yourself. It's easy to be critical and focus on the things we haven't achieved yet, but acknowledging our progress and celebrating what we have accomplished will help us feel gratitude and a level of satisfaction that can only be felt from within. Wherever you are on your path, remember to appreciate just how far you've come, and realize that you need—and deserve—time for yourself just as much as your business and your baby.

After implementing all of these changes in my life I was able to organize my chaos and achieve a level of balance and inner peace that I never had before. This is something I needed to do for myself.

Thankfully—by the grace of God, and the grace of God only—I'm now pregnant.

Please, don't get me wrong. I'm not saying that if a woman is battling infertility, she will get pregnant by solely organizing any chaos she may have in her life the same way I did. But, what I can tell for a fact is that in my case, by letting God be God and focusing back on taking care of myself again, I got out of the way, allowing Him to do what only He can do, and what He does best.

This baby is a miracle from God, deeply cherished and loved.

YOUR TURN:

1. What are your stress triggers?
   _____
   _____

2. How can you organize your day to allocate time for yourself?
   _____
   _____

3. How can you eliminate distractions while you work?
   _____
   _____

4. When was the last time you pampered yourself?
   _____
   _____

TAKEAWAYS:

- When we face situations out of our control, we can rest assured that God is in control.
- Identify, reduce, and eliminate stress triggers.
- Planning your day will help you accomplish more.
- You're still yourself, embrace your individuality.
- This is your journey, focus on the finish line while still enjoying and celebrating the ride.

Draw Your Thoughts

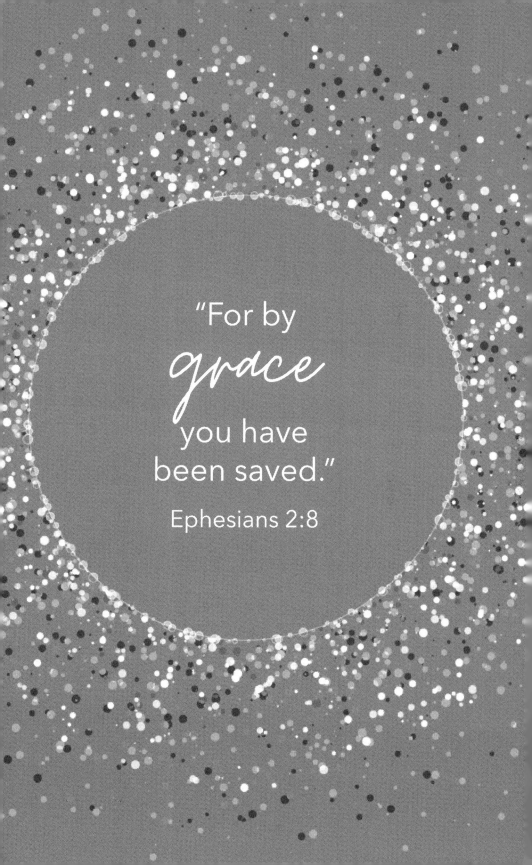

Chapter 9
Win by Grace

In life, there will be times when so much feels overwhelming. Throughout our journey of finding a balance between motherhood and business, every so often we'll do everything right and things may still go wrong. We may give our best and still not be enough. We may feel defeated at times and simply ready to give up.

Changes can drastically affect the perception we have of ourselves and adaptability may not arrive as soon as we need it. Our spark may be dimmed down, clouded by our despair.

The darkness will keep creeping in and growing until we decide it's time to stop it.

Dear one, today is always the day to block the noise, ignite the fire within you, and let yourself glow up through *grace*.

The Aftermath

It's truly remarkable how much our bodies can change during pregnancy and the way it adapts to accommodate the life growing inside of us.

While I was pregnant, there was something about my bump that was enchanting. Honestly, I never felt more beautiful in my life than when I was pregnant; I was truly glowing. I remember touching my belly with love and feeling my baby kicking back in response to my gestures. It's one of the most wonderful memories, and I cherish it with all my heart.

> **And then, my baby was born and my body was no longer the beautiful vessel bearing a life inside of it, but an empty bag that couldn't find its way back to normal.**

Ouch! Those are strong words to say, but that is exactly how I felt at the time.

I was overweight, my feet were swollen, my body was sore, I had deep dark circles under my eyes from sleep deprivation, my hair was falling out from the hormonal changes, and my abdominal skin was saggy from being overstretched. My glow was dim and fading.

People say one of the advantages of breastfeeding for the mother is that you would lose your pregnancy weight very fast. That was not the case for me, in fact, it was quite the opposite. It didn't help of course that I needed to eat certain foods to keep up with my milk supply, and I was also limited in the amount and type of exercises I could do, as I was recovering from a C-Section and I developed Diastasis Recti.

> **It can be ironic in a way, that something as marvelous as creating life can also make us feel like we're not ourselves afterward.**

Unsurprisingly, this whole situation began to weigh on me, and it affected the perception I had of my own beauty and self-love. I remember looking in the mirror and feeling like I didn't recognize the woman staring back at me. What a strange thing to experience. I was going through a very dark phase.

Believe it or not, feeling this way is more common than you may realize and for some, it's not limited to the first few postpartum months. Many veteran moms feel similarly about themselves for years after birthing their children. For some, the sentiment worsens as time passes by. These feelings can be very destructive and it's imperative to address the root of the issue as soon as possible—so how can one overcome such thoughts and emotions?

Giving Yourself Grace

Having a newborn alongside a new business was no easy feat at all, especially when things didn't go according to plan—my birth and postpartum experiences, in particular, are a good representation of that—if anything—not to mention when my stress levels got out of control. Sometimes we can be our worst critics and be too hard on ourselves when we're in the middle of difficult situations. I know I did.

Whenever I'm going through tribulations, I now try to keep my eyes above the waves by fixing my eyes on Jesus. What He says about me is my truth, and He says I'm loved and worth enough to die for, as you are too.

So let's start by reiterating how extraordinary you are. Your body was chosen by God Himself to be His vessel. It endured the unspeakable to create a new life and it went all the way through it to birth your precious baby safe and sound into this world.

Your body is a miracle maker.

Birthing life is a privilege not everyone possesses. You and your body are special, and you should celebrate yourself for accomplishing such a divine task.

Always remember your own value. What you bring to the table for your family, community, profession, and society outweigh any imperfections. Know how exceptional you are by just being *you*, and by doing things exactly the way you do them. You're enough. There's no better mother to your child than you, and your baby loves you because of who *you* are, and that is no one else but yourself.

Comparing the Incomparable

Your personal and professional path is unique and special, try not to compare yourself to others. Avoid scrolling through social media and feeling behind if someone else seems ahead of you in any area. This goes to both your baby and you. Your journey is yours alone and—let's not forget—your definition of success is ultimately the only one that matters.

We are targeted by many different industries around the world to feel less than we are and to constantly be comparing ourselves to what the media defines for us as beautiful. Women's bodies in particular are masterpieces, we come in different gorgeous shapes and forms, and we should love ourselves with our curves as well as our edges.

You're incomparable! The healthiest thing to do is to step away from comparison and focus on enjoying the blessings around us. In reality—as the old saying goes—the grass isn't always greener on the other side of the fence, the grass is greener where *you* water it.

Something you may not have considered is that comparison can be the other way around. Some people will look at you and wish to have the life you're living. What you have may be exactly what the person next door does not, and longs for.

Your ordinary life may be extraordinary to others.

Your attitude and gratitude are everything in this matter. As leaders within our families and communities, we're constantly influencing those around us, whether we realize it or not. It's important to stay positive, be encouraging, and try to uplift others through our own experiences and challenges—what we do and how we do it matters to others. Someone is always watching, especially our little ones.

Slowly but Surely

Define and review your overall goals and organize them by what you can achieve in short-term and long-term periods, so you can appreciate your progress and celebrate your accomplishments as you go. Furthermore, always try to keep your perspective in check.

If there's something you want to change or improve, it's on you to take the first step towards it. Get moving at your own pace. Take one step at a time, even if it's a small one, it will get you in motion.

Usually, the hardest part for me with anything related to health and fitness is to start. If only I get to put my gym clothes on and do the first exercise, then I keep going. The second hardest would be prioritizing it, as working out and eating healthy are usually the first things I tend to sacrifice when any unforeseen situations arise in my daily routine.

Yet, even in these circumstances I try to create an overall equilibrium and focus on my mental health and overall wellbeing. If I miss working out or eat something I shouldn't one day, I don't beat myself up about it anymore. I rest assured I'll try again the next day. Every morning the sun rises up, and it brings with it new opportunities to start over—over and over again.

Listen to your body. Sometimes you will feel like you need to take a break from everything and rest in the middle of the day. If that's the case, just do it. Let others take the lead when needed. As strong and powerful as we are, sometimes taking a pause is all we need in order to keep going.

Nothing changes unless something changes.

As discouraged as you may feel at times, take heart. It's ultimately in your power to make any adjustments and move towards whichever goal you may have for yourself. You are perfectly capable of getting where you want to be. Even if you feel you're advancing too slowly, progress is progress as long as you keep moving forward.

See, life comes with strife and hardship, and that's not necessarily a bad thing.

> **Most of the time our struggles are opportunities from God for us to grow, so we can help others in the future that may go through similar situations.**

Diamonds are formed under pressure, however, they're not formed overnight. It takes time for our bodies to heal and recover, be patient and kind to yourself because everything worthy in life requires dedication, discipline, time, patience, and love and you're the worthiest of them all.

Spend your time and energy appreciating the power within you. We are beautiful, even when our bodies have changed. Giving yourself grace means that as well as with success, *your definition of beautiful is the only one that matters.*

Talk About Your Feelings

Sometimes the simple act of expressing my feelings to someone who can relate to them is enough for me to feel better, as speaking out loud about it tends to take the weight off my shoulders and the sorrow out of my chest. This theory doesn't necessarily apply to every single thing in my life, but many of my problems feel way smaller after I verbally share them with someone I trust. Most of the time this is enough, and I don't even need to take any further action in the matter.

Speaking openly to my husband about my struggles has always helped me find possible solutions for each of them. I get his insight on things and see everything from a different point of view, but most importantly, his compassion and empathy bring the support, comfort, and peace of mind I need.

Yet, sometimes the person we need to speak with is not necessarily our spouse, but someone that can directly relate to what we're going through, or even a professional. This is another reason why expanding your support system outside of your marriage and family's sphere can play a part in the overall outcome of your journey. When talking about our support system, I can say for a fact that the more the merrier.

Allow Yourself to Win

> They say *home is where the heart is*—and my heart is in both architecture and motherhood.

Your love for your career and business may be as passionate as mine, while your fear of the impact motherhood could have on your professional development and aspirations may be as deep as it was for me. Maybe you're already a mom in business and are feeling overwhelmed and just want to give up.

No matter what your situation is or the reason you started this book in the first place, my prayer is that by reading my testimony God has planted a seed inside of you that will grow and produce its fruits in abundance and that my journey made you feel inspired and empowered to take a chance on yourself to strive for anything and everything your heart desires, without exceptions.

Don't let other people's limitations limit you. Block any negativity from being a driving factor in your decision-making. Instead, look at what *you* expect of yourself and the legacy you want to leave behind. Focus on Jesus and yourself. You are the one that can change your life and the world around you for something greater, and you're not alone my friend,

God is with you every step of the way.

He's faithful in His promises and He says in His word:

"Have I not commanded you? Be strong and courageous. Do not be afraid; do not be discouraged, for the Lord your God will be with you wherever you go." Joshua 1:9

"What, then, shall we say in response to these things? If God is for us, who can be against us?" Romans 8:31

With this being the final chapter and as we approach the last few words within this book, I want to acknowledge that even though my experience is based on being the mother of one—and maybe this is your case too or you haven't started on having children yet—it doesn't matter, as nothing in life is settled. My scenario and yours could be altered tomorrow. We need to keep our minds open and embrace any changes that may be thrown our way in the future. Life is in constant movement and as our families grow and/or evolve, we'll face new challenges.

On every page here, I poured my heart out raw and shared with humbleness and vulnerability my reality, struggles, mistakes, failures, accomplishments and victories, and every system I've set up and implemented to accomplish my goals and orchestrate things in harmony.

> **But the ultimate purpose of this book is not to make it about me, but about helping you pave your way to success.**

The intent of every story and advice I'm handing over to you is not to have a one-size-fits-all approach, but to create the footings of a firm foundation to help you stay centered and grounded in the midst of any storm.

This is a blueprint with practical steps to design a glowing balance between motherhood and your career while figuring out what works best for you and your family. Yet—as it happens with any set of plans and construction documents—further action needs to be taken to actually build the design and birth it out into the physical world.

I encourage you to go back to your notes at the end of each chapter and create a list with your goals, spelling out each step you'll be taking moving forward to accomplish them. Circle back and review these notes as many times as needed. It's up to you to take action based on what you've learned here to create your own masterpiece.

As with success and beauty, together with God's definition of things, *your* definition of happiness is the only one that matters. I want you to be enlightened with knowledge, clarity, and direction by understanding your options and the tools available to set you up to live victoriously while you're in the pursuit of your happiness.

Can you hear the roar and feel the flame rushing in from within? Let it burn and spread the light, allow yourself the grace to win.

You can be all. You deserve it all. ***Glow for it!***

YOUR TURN:

1. When did a life-changing event impact your self-esteem?
   _____
   _____

2. What can you do to avoid comparing yourself to others?
   _____
   _____

3. What step can you take today to improve your self-love?
   _____
   _____

4. Who can you talk to about your feelings and struggles?
   _____
   _____

TAKEAWAYS:

- When facing struggles, fix your eyes on Jesus.
- Be kind to yourself.
- Don't compare yourself to others, you're incomparable.
- Any step, big or small, towards your goal is progress.
- You've already won, glow mama, glow!

Draw Your Thoughts

End Notes

Preface

1. National Architectural Accrediting Board. (2020). *Annual Report*. NAAB. https://www.naab.org/wp-content/uploads/2020_NAAB_Annual_Report.pdf
2. National Council of Architectural Registration Boards. (2021). NCARB by the numbers. NCARB. https://www.ncarb.org/nbtn2021/demographics-licensure

Chapter 4

1. Fear. *Merriam-Webster.com Dictionary*. Merriam-Webster. https://www.merriam-webster.com/dictionary/fear

Chapter 5

1. American Institute of Architects. (2020). *Membership Demographics Report*. AIA. https://content.aia.org/sites/default/files/2021-11/2020_Membership_Demographics_Report.pdf
2. American Institute of Architects Tampa Bay. (2020). *Chapter Awards History*. AIA TampaBay. http://www.aiatampabay.com/TPA/Awards_Awards-History.cfm

Chapter 7

1. Taking Cara Babies. (2022). Newborns (0-12 Weeks) *Will I ever sleep again?*. Taking Cara Babies. https://takingcarababies.com/

Acknowledgments

First and foremost, thank you God for paving my path and holding my hand through my entire journey of becoming an architect and a mother. You've always worked in mysterious ways and I wouldn't be here if it wasn't for you. I'm so thankful for your infinite love and grace.

    To my husband Jeremy. Thank you for always believing in me and for encouraging me to always reach for more. It blows my mind how God designed us for each other. You're my perfect match. Thank you for being my biggest supporter, and for riding the wave of my crazy ideas. Thank you for being my best friend, and for loving me in a way so deep and pure that I still cannot comprehend. I'm the lucky one of the two of us!

    To Nova. Thank you for transforming this architect into an Archimom. You've given me the greatest title I've ever earned, this is the one that makes me the proudest. Being your mother is something I consider a badge of honor. You've taught me the highest meaning of love and selflessness. I am a better woman, architect, leader, and business owner because of you. I want you to know that I was reborn with you on June 15, 2020, and every day since I've learned more from you than from anyone or anything else. Thank you for giving me the privilege of being your mommy. Watching you grow is the biggest blessing in my life.

There's nothing more important than you. I love you recklessly and infinitely, my sweet girl.

To my mother Daysi and my sister Paola. Thank you both for being my biggest protectors, advocates, and role models to look up to since I was little. The fact that you both were able to raise your children as single moms while being successful women in the workforce makes me feel such a deep sense of respect and admiration for your strengths, dedication, and commitment to yourselves and your family. I love you both more than I can express.

To my father Ramon, my stepmother Engracia, and my five younger brothers Ramoncito, José, Manuel, César, and Néstor. Thank you for your love, encouragement, and unconditional support! Each one of you makes my life complete.

To my Kloter family: Sandy, Darryl, Shawn, Lindsey, Jason, Cory, Dean, Trent, Barry, Joyce, Kent, Janell, and Linda. Thank you for becoming my family and filling out the gaps in my life since I left my home country.

To my Young Architect family: Michael, Courtney, Joanna, Destiny, and Chad. Thank you for your continued support every step of my career in the US. I wouldn't be here without you.

To my LEAP Group family: Luciana, Mariela, Mercedes, Muna, Shannon, MJ, Emma, Christine, Ashley, Sheila, Leslie, Meeta, and Tamara. Thank you for giving me the privilege of being a part of this amazing group, and for your unconditional support, advice, and guidance in so many different areas of my personal life, professional growth, and the development of Glow Architects. I'm continuously learning from each one of you, and you inspire me to reach for more and be my best in everything I do.

To Graciela, Joann, Mandy, Emily, Lourdes, Nati, Kim and Beverly. Thank you for your selfless support toward my career advancement, but most importantly, thank you for leading by example. Your advocacy continuously inspires so many of us who look up to you as role models.

To the WIA Tampa Bay Committee. Thank you for giving your time, efforts, and talents to serve our community and for taking our mission to the next level. Everything we do has a ripple effect on the lives and career paths of the wonderful women in architecture around us.

To Jackie, Lillian, Sara, Cassie, Esther, Jennifer, Gianna, Yocelsys, Meggie, Julin, and all the other mothers and friends in my inner circle. Thank you for being there when I needed you the most, without expecting anything in return.

I love you all!

Sincerely,

Gloria Kloter, AIA, NCARB, CODIA

About the Author

Gloria Kloter, AIA, NCARB, CODIA, is an award-winning architect, founder and CEO of Glow Architects, a keynote speaker, and a bestselling author. Gloria has been a practicing architect both in her home country (Dominican Republic) and in the United States since 2004. She is an advocate for immigrant architects, women in architecture, and motherhood.

Kloter has dedicated a huge chunk of her career to helping other young architects grow. As a leader in the architecture community, she is the founder of the Foreign Architects, a private online community where she mentors young and aspiring immigrant architects on how to obtain their architect license in the United States.

As a testament to her influence and impact, Gloria Kloter has served as the Architect Licensing Advisor of the State of Florida through AIA Florida. She has also served as part of the Board of Directors of the AIA Tampa Bay where she is the founding chairperson of the Women in Architecture (WIA) committee.

Among her awards and recognitions, Gloria is a recipient of the Outstanding Leadership Award 2022 by Realty 2.0 and the AIA Tampa Bay 2020 Kelley Emerging Professional Award. She was also honored with the 2019 Sho-Ping Ching Women's Leadership Summit Scholarship, a recognition to mid-career women architects who are advancing toward leadership roles and are making a positive impact within their communities.

Gloria has been a keynote speaker and panelist on several occasions at the Young Architect conference, NCARB's Architect Licensing Advisor Summit, AIA National Conference on Architecture, Women Architects Festival, World Creativity and Innovation Conference, AIA Western Mountain Region Vision 2020, Realty 2.0, among other events.

Gloria Kloter and Glow Architects have been featured by major architectural and global publications like Architizer, The Young Architect Podcast, The Context & Clarity Podcast, Arquitexto, NCARB, YAF Connection, South Tampa Magazine, Thrive Global, Tech Times, Influencive, and others, regarding her experience in the field of Architecture, Interior Design, her volunteer work, and her journey as a foreign architect in the USA.

Made in United States
Orlando, FL
09 June 2022